D1547389

TEACHING
LITERATURE

KRC
2013

TEACHING LITERATURE

A Seventh-day Adventist Approach

DELMER DAVIS

The Robert Arthur Williams Library
Florida Hospital College of Health Sciences
800 Lake Estelle Drive
Orlando, Florida 32803

PN
61
D39
2002

ANDREWS UNIVERSITY PRESS
BERRIEN SPRINGS, MI

©2002 by Andrews University Press
213 Information Services Building
Berrien Springs, MI 49104-1700   U.S.A.
Tel: 269-471-6134; Fax: 269-471-6224
info@andrewsuniversitypress.com
http://www.andrewsuniversitypress.com

All rights reserved. No part of this publication may be reproduced, stored in a retrieval system, or transmitted in any form or by any means, electronic, mechanical, photocopying, recording, or otherwise, without the prior permission of the copyright owner.

Printed in the United States of America
06 05 04 03 02   5 4 3 2 1

Library of Congress Cataloging-in-Publication Data

Davis, Delmer, 1939-
   Teaching literature : a Seventh-day Adventist approach / Delmer Davis.
      p. cm.
   Includes bibliographical references and index.
   ISBN 1-883925-36-3
   1. Literature--Study and teaching (Secondary)--United States. 2.
Literature--Study and teaching (Higher)--United States. 3. Religion and
literature. I. Title.

PN61 .D39 2002
807'.1'173--dc21
                              2002028351

Editing   Deborah Everhart
Cover Design   Matt Hamel
Text Design   Nathaniel Stearman

Publication of this book has been sponsored by:

The Institute for Christian Teaching
Department of Education
General Conference of Seventh-day Adventists
12501 Old Columbia Pike
Silver Spring, MD 20904   U.S.A.
rodrigueze@gc.adventist.org

The Center for College Faith
Andrews University
Berrien Springs, MI 49104   U.S.A.
kutzner@andrews.edu, randy@andrews.edu

TABLE OF CONTENTS

FOREWORD

In one of His memorable sayings, Jesus elaborated on an earlier revelation by stating that our first priority in life is to love God with all our being—heart, soul, strength, and mind (Mark 12:30, NIV). He thus challenged His disciples then and through the centuries to engage their intellect in an enduring conversation with and devotion to God. This is rational love—rooted in faith, nurtured in obedience, and demanding a commitment to truth anchored on certain fundamental premises: All truth is of God; Jesus Christ is the incarnate Word of truth; the Holy Spirit leads us to all truth; and the Scriptures are the written Word of truth.

Such affirmations sound counter-cultural in an age that has relativized truth, fragmented knowledge, and enthroned human beings as their own moral arbiters. Yet this situation is not entirely new. Almost twenty centuries ago the Apostle Paul—a committed Christian intellectual—challenged believers not to "conform any longer to the pattern of this world, but to be transformed by the renewing of your mind" (Rom. 12:2). Since education is one of the great molders of the worldview and values of the next generation, any endeavor to help young men and women learn to think *Christianly* necessarily involves teachers and mentors who think and model *Christianly*.

The new century offers Christian educators a fresh opportunity to reflect deeply on the coherence between their faith and their teaching. In particular, Seventh-day Adventist teachers should take an inventory of what they believe and how that belief governs and permeates their teaching. Such an evaluation would lead to an examination of their interaction with students inside and outside the classroom, and how that interaction helps students develop a Christian-biblical worldview on which they will base their life priorities and moral choices. Students in Christian colleges and universities will be encouraged to reject the dualism of our culture that separates faith from learning, knowledge from values, and belief from behavior. They will understand that a commitment to truth is not limiting but liberating (John 8:32) and that, for the Christian, life on this planet is the beginning of a broad educational experience that will embrace time and eternity.

The integration of faith and learning, then, is not an option to those in the Christian learning experience. It is an intentional and systematic process of approaching the entire educational enterprise—curricular and co-curricular, individual and collective—from a biblical perspective. Its aim is to ensure that students, under the influence of committed Christian teachers and by the time they leave school, will have freely internalized biblical values and a view of life, knowledge, and destiny that is Christ-centered, service-oriented, and kingdom-directed.

This integration must be seen not as a destination but as a journey that lasts as long as we live. The teacher's self-confidence will be tempered by humility, recognizing that we "now see a poor reflection," but that some day "we shall see face to face," and that although "now I know in part; then I shall know fully, even as I am fully known" (1 Cor. 13:12).

The co-sponsors of this publishing project—The Institute for Christian Teaching (a service of the Department of Education of the General Conference of Seventh-day Adventists) and The Center for College Faith at Andrews University—fervently desire that this series will encourage Christian teachers in other disciplines to reflect upon the relationship between their faith and their intellectual endeavors, seeking interconnections, coherence, and wholeness. Such an activity not only counteracts the tragic secularization of contemporary higher education but also invigorates their teaching and, we hope, results in additional contributions to the growing body of literature on the integration of faith and learning.

> Humberto M. Rasi, Director
> Department of Education
> General Conference of Seventh-day Adventists

PREFACE

Seventh-day Adventist teachers of literature have long participated in exploring the relationship of their faith to their discipline. In general, these explorations have centered on clarifying how particular texts or genres can or should be taught, in spite of apparent prohibitions inherent in the conservative Seventh-day Adventist religious heritage. During the last half-century, however, developments in literary theory have raised serious questions about the basic premises of Christianity in general and have made it necessary for Christian literary critics, including Seventh-day Adventists, to address issues that in the past were taken for granted. Indeed, a number of Christian teachers of literature have called for the development of what Clarence Walhout has termed a "'Christian literary theory' to stand on equal terms" with other contemporary approaches to literature (Walhout, "Introduction" vii).

This book brings together Christian and, more specifically, Seventh-day Adventist attitudes regarding the teaching of literature. My premise in writing the book has been that the most important contribution I could make to the Seventh-day Adventist classroom teaching of literature would be to raise issues and synthesize responses, with particular emphasis on the challenges of contemporary literary theory. This book is meant to be introductory, however, and does not provide final answers. It does not present a definitive Seventh-day Adventist solution as to exactly how to integrate faith and the teaching of literature. What the book does do is to provide a basis upon which further conversations can take place. By bringing together the attitudes and thoughts of the most important Christian and Seventh-day Adventist writers about literature, moreover, the book provides easy access to materials which in the past have not been readily available to many Seventh-day Adventist literature teachers.

The book does not provide specific ideas regarding methods of teaching literature. It does not list strategies regarding what to do in the classroom on Monday morning. Instead, my purpose has been to probe the larger questions behind the teaching of literature which every Seventh-day Adventist teacher of literature must inevitably face: What is literature and why teach literature (Chapter 1)? What is literary theory and why does contemporary literary theory present particular challenges for Christians (Chapter 2)? What is the relationship of Christian faith to teaching and reading literature (Chapter 3)? What are the particular questions about literature raised by Seventh-day Adventists (Chapter 4)? Is there still reason to teach the Bible as literature in the Seventh-day Adventist classroom (Chapter 5)? Why should literary theory and literary criticism matter to Seventh-day Adventists (Chapter 6)?

My experience as a teacher of literature has centered almost exclusively on texts in English as a result of my education and lifetime career in the United States. Thus, the works and writers cited throughout the book are mostly American or British. In spite of this limitation, teachers of literature in languages other than English in nations throughout the world should be able to adapt the ideas in this book to their own cultures and heritages.

I have used the standard "in-text" documentation system of the Modern Language Association throughout the book, with footnotes reserved for content explanations and clarifications. Full bibliographical information is included in the "Works Cited" pages at the end of the book. Many of the works listed there, however, are also included with annotations in the "Further Reading" section of the book.

I look forward to hearing reactions to this book from readers throughout the world as they think through the issues raised in considering how to think Christianly about the teaching of literature. If the book stimulates such conversations, then it will have accomplished much of its main purpose.

Delmer Davis
Department of English
Andrews University
Berrien Springs, MI 49104 U.S.A.
davisd@andrews.edu

CHAPTER ONE

INTRODUCTION: WHAT IS LITERATURE AND WHY READ IT?

"Literature" is not easily defined. Even such a formidable critic as Northrop Frye notes that it would be impossible "to write an elementary textbook expounding" the "fundamental principles" of literature and literary criticism because such a book could "not start with a clear answer to the first question of all: 'What is literature?' We have," says Frye, "no real standards to distinguish a verbal structure that is literary from one that is not [...]" (*Anatomy* 13).

I tested Frye's premise out recently on the first day of a literary analysis course when I asked twenty students to write their definitions of literature. Predictably, the responses varied considerably. In perhaps the best answer of all, one student chided me for posing an unfair question since literature was something that could not be defined in a brief class exercise. Another student expressed that literature is "something long, tedious and boring." Most students, doubtless vaguely recalling past literature courses, mentioned such words as "classic," "artistic," "creative," and "lasting over time." A couple of respondents emphasized that in order for writing to be "literature," readers must be moved and emotionally caught up in a "communion" that is almost "magical." Finally, a few students underscored that literature must communicate "insights," "meaning," and "truths" about experience. In spite of the variance and inconsistency in these student responses, what is fascinating is that, as a group, the students touched on most of the points usually mentioned by experienced literary critics as they attempt to wrestle with the same task.

Dictionary definitions of "literature" explain that the English word "literature" comes from a Latin term *littera*, meaning letter. Related Latin words center on reading, writing, and being educated; hence, our modern term "literacy." Indeed, in the history of the word in English, "literature" originally referred quite generally to all things written. Something

1

of the same meaning exists in the Seventh-day Adventist tradition of referring to the door-to-door salespeople of denominational books and journals as literature evangelists.

Over the recent centuries, however, with the development of modern literary criticism and the increasing centrality of literature study throughout all educational levels, the meaning of the word has become somewhat more specialized, centering most often on writing that is imaginative or creative. Frye, in *The Educated Imagination*, a work attempting to convince the reader of the importance of literature, explores the differences between the language of the utilitarian, "practical" realms of life and the language of the world of literature, noting it is the "imagination, which produces the literary language of poems and plays and novels" (21, 23). Frye emphasizes that such writing (or literature) is an artistic, imaginative construction "of possible models of human experience" (22).

Most recent introductory literature anthologies take for granted that the term "literature" relates almost exclusively to works of the imagination. Laurie G. Kirszner and Stephen R. Mandell, for example, begin their section entitled "What is Literature" in *Literature: Reading, Reacting, Writing* with an explanation of what "imaginative literature" is. As the authors note, "writers of imaginative literature often manipulate facts—change dates, invent characters, and create dialogue." Such writers also "include words chosen not only because they communicate the writer's ideas, but also because they are memorable." Imaginative writing, including "vivid imagery," "evocative comparisons," and "multiple connotations of words," makes it possible for "imaginative literature [...] to stretch language to its limits" and to "suggest many possible interpretations" (1).

This emphasis upon the language of literature, of course, is closely linked to the aesthetic or artistic dimensions of literature, facets usually touched on in most standard definitions and noted even by my students in the literary analysis course. That the best imaginative literature should be regarded as artistic is something that most critics can agree upon and that those artistic qualities have something to do with the way the writer uses language and structural options in order to create the text is also generally not disputed. Harold Bloom asserts, for example, that "one breaks into the canon only by aesthetic strength, which is constituted primarily of an amalgam: mastery of figurative language, originality, cognitive power, knowledge, exuberance of diction" (29). What is under dispute—and what may always be under dispute—is which texts possess the requisite artistic dimensions to qualify as literature (embodying issues of the canon, which will be explored later) or, even more fundamentally, what qualifies as art in any particular work of literature. Courses such as literary analysis and countless introductory textbooks on literature are the educational establishment's attempts to equip readers with the requisite skills and insights to make aesthetic judgments about the imaginative literature they read.

Besides noting the aesthetic qualities in literature, the students in my literary analysis class also touched on what they termed "insights," "meaning," and "truths." Inevitably, perhaps, as a class of Christian students, such concerns would surface. What is important to remember, however, is that most critics, regardless of philosophical or religious premises, share this same concern in one way or another, although many contemporary literary scholars probably would not be comfortable with the word "truths." Even Bloom, who seemingly admires Oscar Wilde's stance that "art is perfectly useless," goes ahead to underscore that the "West's greatest writers are subversive of all values [...]" (16, 29), thus admitting an important meaning element in literary works of art, the sort of approach to content concerns raised by Kirszner and Mandell when they emphasize that the best fiction "often goes against the grain, challenging cherished beliefs and leading readers to reexamine long-held assumptions" (12).

A final element noted by a couple of students in my class centers on the experience of the reader when reading literature, what was termed by them as a sort of "magical" "communion" of reader with text or reader with writer. Most literary critics treat such responses as the element of pleasure or enjoyment that results from being caught up in the literature-reading experience. Alexander Pope's eighteenth-century poem, "Essay on Criticism," echoes the Roman writer Horace who linked meaning to pleasure by insisting that poetry should not only "inform" but also "delight" (Bate 56). Kirszner and Mandell emphasize that "literature should touch you on a deep emotional or intellectual level, and if it does not—despite its technical perfection—it fails to achieve one of its primary aims" (14). When readers undergo a positive response to literature, that reaction, note James H. Pickering and Jeffrey D. Hoeper, accompanies a "sense of pleasure or delight, in much the same way that we respond to a painting, a piece of sculpture, or a musical composition" (4).

So difficult has it been for literary critics and scholars to define specifically what literature is that many leap immediately to descriptions of the categories or genres of imaginative writing as a way of supplying a clarifying map of the literary territory. Typically, three major genres are described: poetry, drama, and fiction. Often, a fourth category is touched on: non-fiction prose. Of course, many subcategories of literature exist within each of the major categories, with each subdivision needing definition and characterization. Poetry, for example, includes such important subcategories as the epic, dramatic poetry, and lyric poetry; and these categories can be subdivided even further. Within lyric poetry are such types as the sonnet, the elegy, and the ballad, to name but a few. Fiction includes at least two major subdivisions—the novel and the short story—but can be further subdivided into such types as the romance, the western, the detective story, or the gothic. Drama includes the major categories of comedy and tragedy, but also numerous varieties of each. While defining each of these categories may be almost as challenging as defining literature itself, the value to emphasizing the genres in a classroom consideration of the term "literature" is that most readers immediately can conjure up some past experience with examples from the various genres and can, therefore, begin a discussion of the elements of each genre in a more productive way than when tackling the larger question of what literature itself is.

Why Read Literature?

Often, discussions of what literature is inevitably overlap into issues regarding the purpose of literature. Why read imaginative writing? What do readers get from the experience? Most responses to these questions can be grouped under two headings: enjoyment and insight. Horace emphasized both in his *Ars Poetica,* insisting that poetry will "delight or enlighten the reader,/ Or say what is both amusing and really worth using" (qtd. from Richter, *Critical* 75).

That literature can be pleasure-giving has already been noted as a major quality of the definition of imaginative writing. But what kind of pleasure does literature provide its audience? Here the responses are varied. Aristotle emphasizes the emotionally purgative experience of tragedy as the emotions of pity and fear are sloughed away during the course of a drama, resulting in a balancing of the emotions, a sort of pleasurable stasis. Quintilian centers on how literature can "move the audience" and "arouse a strong emotional response," resulting in "pleasure" (Danziger and Johnson 11). At the extreme are those who praise literature's ability to move to the extent that it can "take readers where they have never been before" (Kirsner and Mandell 2), resulting, perhaps, in the readers' loss of their "own sense of identity" (Danziger and Johnson 11). Most writers about literature, however, emphasize that with the best literature the pleasure of such nearly complete identification is followed by new insights into life experiences which the literature also provides. This emphasis on literature as providing the pleasure of "meaningful escape" is countered by others who insist that the enjoyment of literature is most wrapped up in the reader's constant sense of the literary creation's artifice or constructed nature and that it is the objective enjoyment (in contrast to subjective identification) of those created artistic features that most defines the pleasure involved in experiencing literature (Danziger and Johnson 11).

Just as the enjoyment of literature runs a gambit from the pleasures of escape to those of artistic analysis, so there is considerable divergence as to what kinds of instruction or insights literature provides. What does Horace mean when he emphasizes the poet's need "to enlighten the reader"? Few would subscribe today to the idea that literature so represents life and how it is to be led that imaginative reading should become a sort of moral guide to behavior, no matter how tempting that view may be to conservative Christians as they evaluate their reading. Edgar Roberts and Henry Jacobs, however, catalogue a lengthy and constructive list of values, which reading literature can provide, ending with the following summation: "Through our cumulative experience in reading, literature shapes our goals and values [...]. It enables us to develop perspectives on events occurring locally and globally, and thereby it gives us understanding and control. It is one of the shaping influences of life. It makes us human" (1-2). As grandiose and all-encompassing as such generalizations may seem to be, many serious literature teachers, regardless of their religious commitment and in spite of certain recent critical approaches to reading that seemingly erode confidence in the reliability of any insights gained from literary study, continue to subscribe to the belief that literature "can enable readers to see their lives and times more clearly" (Kirsner and Mandrell 2-3). These insights are more than lessons or morals or messages. The total effect of the reading of an imaginative piece of literature, a work which combines content and form in a seamless artifice, is that the audience partakes of the "world or vision" of the work and the "interpretation of life that has been achieved [...]" (Danziger and Johnson 17).

CHAPTER TWO

LITERARY THEORY AND ISSUES OF THE CANON[1]

Although there may be some general agreement about what literature is and what the major benefits of reading literature are, disputes arise regarding how readers should approach literary texts and with what assumptions. Such disputes grow out of philosophical differences about how art is created and the relationship of a literary work to the author, the reader, the world of reality, and the world of art traditions and conventions. What follows is a brief overview of some of the major approaches to reading and understanding literature over the centuries. Such an overview is important for the Christian who must evaluate the underlying premises of these approaches in light of a world view that places God at the center of the universe and at the core of all meaning. The overview is organized into three phases: pre-modernism, modernism, and postmodernism, categories used by James Sire in his book *The Universe Next Door: A Basic Worldview Catalog* (175). For Sire, pre-modernism is characterized first by an emphasis on being, with being, for theists, anchored in belief in the existence of God. Thinking and knowing grow out of this emphasis on being (176). Modernism, in contrast, emphasizes thinking first, as exemplified in Descartes' famous "I think, therefore I am" dictum. Sire ties this emphasis on thinking to the growth of scientific rationalism and the Enlightenment, the movement away from the "authority of the ancients" to a dependence on "human reason" to find "truth" (176-177). In literary theory, modernism is equated with twentieth-century attempts to approach literature

---

[1] Often, the terms "literary criticism" and "literary theory" are used almost interchangeably. It is perhaps well, however, to keep some distinctions in mind. Literary theory is generally understood to be "the principles and assumptions" which guide the literary critic in analyzing and interpreting texts (Murfin and Ray 400-01). Literary criticism is a broader term that can include attention to theory but more likely centers on the actual application of theory to specific texts (64).

rationally and objectively, with the "scientific" rigor first emphasized during the Enlightenment. Modern approaches to literature do not question the validity of finding meaning in language and in texts and generally assume that all readers, given the right experience, will agree on such meaning. Postmodernism, in contrast, questions the interpretive reliability of so-called "rational" approaches to understanding reality, emphasizing that interpretations are really only subjective linguistic responses. As Sire notes, postmodernism centers on how language constructs knowing and on how language does not guarantee any reliable relationship to reality (177-179). In Bressler's words, "Truth itself is relative, depending on the various cultural and social influences in one's life" (118). Since language forms meaning or what passes for truth, truth has become what works, what is most powerful. As Sire observes, "There is no purely objective knowledge, no truth of correspondence. Instead, there are only stories, stories which, when they are believed, give the storyteller power over others." Thus, "we create truth as we construct languages that serve our purposes" (180-181).

Pre-Modernism

The Historical Approach

Prior to the Romantic writers and theorists of the nineteenth century, few literary scholars questioned how literature should be approached. Most agreed with both Plato and Aristotle that literature is mimetic, that is, an imitation of life or reality, and, thus, is grounded, however tenuously from Plato's point of view, in a relationship to the orderly universe as it exists, to history or to the events of life (Bressler 17-21). Christian thinkers and writers merged the Greco-Roman views of reality with a Christian theology that puts God at the center of the universe, working out His plans for humanity through the events of history. The historical approach to reading a work of literature attempts to uncover the conditions surrounding the work when it was written, including attention to the author's life, concerns, and writing purposes, as well as the events and preoccupations of the society within which the author lived (Guerin et al. 22). As Bressler notes, although a pervasive and seemingly obvious approach to meaning for centuries, perhaps the most succinct and structured statements promoting the historical approach came from Hippolyte Taine, the nineteenth-century French literary critic, who emphasized that to understand a literary text one must consider the "influences" of "race, milieu, and moment." These influences include the author's life sequence and "personal characteristics," the environment in which the author produced the text, and the events of the time surrounding the author's work. When these influences and the text are examined together, then the reader understands that "no text is written in a vacuum, but is instead the result of history" (29).

This historical approach to understanding literature dominated Western literary thinking for centuries and continued to be an important force in literary studies as universities and colleges multiplied in Western Europe, England, and the United States during the latter part of the nineteenth century and the early part of the twentieth century. Even what has usually been regarded as the nineteenth-century "philological approach" to literature (commonly associated with an emphasis on the scientific study of the language of a literary text) was, indeed, a part of the historical approach in that such language studies usually attempted to reveal the original meanings of words or syntax and depended on a developmental model or history of the language approach to texts. As Gerald Graff notes, moreover, the philological approach, understood in its most complete way, included all aspects of reality related to a text and its environment, not just its language, including, for example, "'geography, political history, customs […]'" (69).

The Moralistic/Philosophical Approach

Hand in hand with the traditional historical approach to understanding a literary text is the moralistic/philosophical approach to meaning. As Bressler notes, Plato's reservations about poetry rested on his concerns that the imitative qualities of literature are at best third-rate, because poetry depends on intuitive responses to a reality (the world around the author) which in itself is but an imitation of the eternal truths upon which the universe rests. It is the tenuousness of poetry's truth-telling that bothered Plato. He never argues with the essential "given" that literature attempts to tell truth or provide insights for listeners and readers to follow (17-18). More positive in his approach to the worth of meaning in literature was Aristotle who elevates poetry's truth-telling to a high level of reliability in his emphasis on how imaginative works attempt to reveal the "universal" as opposed to history which centers on "the particular" (19). Since Horace's linking of delight and instruction as major goals for literature, few individuals prior to the twentieth century have seriously questioned the idea that literature provides insights into the moral necessities of life. James Vanden Bosch emphasizes that "moral critics seem to agree on at least two basic assumptions […] first, that works of literature may have moral content, and second, that literature thus has, at least potentially, implications for the moral life of readers" (48-49). Reading literature for truth about how to live means a close examination of the text for its essential meanings plus a relating of those meanings to one's own value system. Very often, this analysis results in an attempt to uncover the philosophical ideas upon which the text is based, thus placing the text within the flow of the history of ideas (Guerin et al. 25-26).

Such an approach has been particularly attractive to Christians through the ages as they have attempted to discover the place of art in their spiritual lives. Unfortunately, often Christians have been so focused on their own beliefs and values that their insistence on the moral dimensions of literature has too easily dismissed even the most didactic of non-Christian writings, regardless of their aesthetic qualities or basic, if incomplete, congruence with Christian ideals. Leland Ryken, the Christian literary critic, argues against this narrow understanding of how many Christians approach works of art, suggesting that they can benefit from works of literature built around world views quite opposed to their own belief system. Ryken notes that "the value of the arts is not that they necessarily or always teach truth." Rather, contact with the arts by Christians results in "supplying the material upon which the Christian mind can apply Christian principles," resulting in "a catalyst to thinking" (*Liberated* 148).

Modernism

Formalism (The New Criticism)

The traditional approaches to understanding literary texts flourished until the early part of the twentieth century. With the growth of scientific rationalism and the accompanying erosion of traditional belief systems in Western culture, however, scholars and critics inevitably began to question the dominant world view inherent in the Judaic/Christian religions and revealed in Western culture's traditional historical and moralistic approaches to literary study. Could not literature be approached more fairly and more reliably—in fact, more scientifically—if the preconceptions of the past about the importance of history and morality were dispensed with and the texts were looked at objectively and rigorously? The result was the emergence of formalism, usually referred to in America as "the New Criticism," a critical stance which especially dominated American literary culture during the 1930s, 40s, and 50s. In part a reaction against the "subjective" or "impressionistic" readings of texts in the historical and moralistic/philosophical traditions of literary criticism, the "New Critics" attempted an unbiased approach to understanding texts. New Criticism or formalism elevates the literary text to a supreme position, an object to be analyzed and understood by applying rigid principles and tools of analysis. This approach rejects the so-called "extrinsic" methods of understanding literature—details from history, the author's biography, intentions, and beliefs, or the reader's philosophical or moral premises. The New Critics were convinced that a "close reading," employing an objective approach, could search out the meaning inherent in the text, including whatever that text had to say about moral, political, or social issues (Graff 145-149).

Essential to the close readings of texts emphasized by the New Critics is the analysis of words, language use, rhetorical figures, literary texture, and structure. In contrast to later literary critics, formalistic approaches never questioned that a text intends to mean and that meaning can be understood. Such critics agreed that good literary works are aesthetically unified and provide meaning, even if that unity and meaning is achieved through seemingly contradictory and paradoxical literary elements within the text. Indeed, the close readings of texts tended to elevate densely-written and complex works to high importance in the literary canon, since such texts provided the richest possibilities for careful analysis. This was the era in which the difficult and image-rich metaphysical English poetry of the seventeenth century (by, for example, John Donne and George Herbert) rose to new prominence because of its possibilities for analysis of paradox and ambiguity (Guerin et al. 70-87).

Typical issues a formalistic critic emphasizes about a text include the following: word connotations, denotations; allusions; images, symbols, figures of speech; structural patterns; tone; theme; point of view; paradox; and irony.[2] Very importantly, the New Critics believed that the objective analysis of a literary work, using formalistic tools, would inevitably uncover the best interpretation of a literary text. In this sense, they subscribed to the idea that there is only one "single best interpretation" for any work (Tyson 132).

Later critics have pointed out the limitations of the formalistic approach to meaning. The New Critics' emphasis on careful analysis, built around the assumption of unity in a text, works best on "short poems and stories" since

---

[2] See Bressler 46-47 for a useful set of questions to ask when approaching a text from a formalistic perspective.

"the shorter the text, the more of its formal elements could be analyzed" (Tyson 132). Longer works tended to receive only partial readings from the New Critics. The insistence, moreover, upon an objective analysis short-changes the reader's emotional investment in the aesthetic experience and what "the text *does*" to its reader (Tyson 154). Also, the stance that a literary text has only one best reading seems to ignore the reality of how readers contribute to meaning in the reading process, how cultures help to determine the meaning of any text, and how different historical time periods affect understandings of literary works and language (Guerin et al. 365). Finally, the very objectivity of the New Critics has been questioned. In the United States, for example, it is clear in retrospect that the New Critics shared certain politically conservative, racially exclusive, and largely agrarian attitudes which inevitably colored their critical pronouncements about texts and undercut their claims to lack of bias in approaching literary texts (Graff 148-151).

Even with these shortcomings, however, one cannot ignore the important contributions which formalism provided to later critical movements. It continues to be a rich approach for the classroom in that it provides specific tools and methods for beginning readers to come to an understanding of literature (Bressler 45-46). More importantly, all the later critical approaches depend to some extent on close readings of texts as a method of providing evidence for their perspectives, even if their basic assumptions about literary meaning diverge considerably from those of the New Critics (Tyson 133). And for the Christian, as Leland Ryken has pointed out, formalistic criticism has in general provided a reasonably comfortable approach to understanding literary texts since, even though it disclaims any overt ties to theology and religion, its high regard for language and meaning, for images, for aesthetic beauty and unity, and for creative design all can be linked to Christian understandings of God-given creativity and how creativity functions in human beings created in His image ("Formalist" 15-20). Formalism for the Christian also provides an "acceptable" nod to modern science in its insistence upon rigor in literary analysis. Also, the fact that the most influential pioneers of this method of literary study were politically and religiously conservative and that T. S. Eliot, perhaps the most influential English poet of the twentieth century, claimed by the New Critics as at minimum a "fellow traveler," embraced Christianity in the late 1920s, may have provided a certain comfort for Christian literary scholars during the domination of the New Criticism.

Structuralism

Sometimes confused with formalistic approaches to literature, structuralism owes much of its theoretical groundings to the linguistic theories of the early twentieth-century French linguist, Ferdinand de Saussure, who emphasized that all languages are ordered by systems or recurrent patterns from which individual utterances emerge (Tyson 201). Connections between words and objects or concepts are arbitrary relationships integral to language systems. Meaning in language is tied to our ability to perceive differences among utterances based on our developmental (and often "unconscious") knowledge of the language system to which we belong.

Saussure's influential theories about language as a system have been applied to other areas of human experience that give themselves to analysis as systems or structures. Semiotics, for example, centers on "non-linguistic objects and behaviors," attempting to find underlying patterns which increase our understanding of the realities of human experience (Tyson 205). Structural anthropologists attempt to examine the unifying elements that unite human cultures (Tyson 204). Similarly, literary critics, influenced by a systems' approach, attempt to discover the common elements or systems which unify texts or genres.

European structuralism centered efforts in particular on examining the similar technical patterns found in narrative texts, analyzing the similar structures that are found universally in folk and fairy tales, for example. The European structuralists developed intricate models from their study of story, specifically noting the various structural phases or parts that narratives reveal and constructing models by which an individual story may be analyzed in relationship to the general narrative patterns (Bressler 97-98). In the rigor of these analyses, structuralism has much in common with formalism, the main difference being the tendency of the structuralists to be interested in what many literary texts hold in common rather than centering on any particular text and its particular meaning (Bressler 94-95).

Related to structuralism (some would say a division of structuralism[3]), the so-called archetypal or mythological approach to literature, spear-headed

---

[3] Some authorities would not label archetypal criticism as a part of structuralism, but would instead emphasize the similarities between the two approaches and would place archetypal criticism within the psychological approach to texts. See, for example, Bressler 148-49, 154-55.

by Frye, attempts to uncover the underlying mythic patterns of texts. This approach to a unifying vision of literature is somewhat based on Carl Jung's psychological theories about the "collective unconscious shared" by "the human family" (Guerin et al. 177). The myths or stories of a culture express the deepest "instinctual life" of a people, and yet also show similarities in "motifs or themes" across cultures. "Such motifs and images are called *archetypes* [...] universal symbols" (Guerin et al. 159-160). Frye, in his *Anatomy of Criticism* and other critical writings, bringing together psychological and anthropological insights, organized these patterns, motifs, and symbols into a complex and all-encompassing structural theory of literature which connects various literary genres to seasonal archetypes, thus demonstrating the unity of literary texts while at the same time making provision for their variations.

Like the New Criticism in its claim to a "scientific" approach to understanding texts, structuralism has been a highly influential approach for Christians to embrace in their attempt to utilize modern theory in understanding literature. Structuralism, as Tremper Longman III notes, has been of "major importance in contemporary research on the Old and New Testaments," much more so than the New Criticism (27). Perhaps this is the result of the European origin of the approach and the fact that biblical studies continue to flourish in Europe. Finally, Northrop Frye's emphasis on the importance of the Scriptures, as underscored by such a work as *The Great Code: The Bible and Literature*, his highly-regarded study of the Bible as literature, has made his particular brand of literary theory and criticism particularly useful to Christian scholars.[4]

Reader-Response Criticism

Although somewhat contemporary with New Criticism and structuralism in its roots, reader-response criticism failed to achieve the influence of the formalistic and structuralist approaches to literature prior to the 1970s. Only in more recent decades has the reader-response approach become popular as a method of discovering meaning. Somewhat rooted in phenomenology, reader-response theory rests on the premise that knowledge and meaning does not

---

[4] See, for example, Leland Ryken's *The Literature of the Bible*. Also, of interest to Seventh-day Adventists, note Minon Hamm's doctoral dissertation, *Anatomy of the Center: An Application of Some Concepts of Northrop Frye*, in which she applies Frye's archetypal structuralism to the Bible's *Song of Songs*.

exist independently of the perceiver or the human "consciousness" (Bressler 71). Reading theory builds on this premise by suggesting that in a reading situation, two elements are essential: a text and a reader of the text. Without a reader, however, no text has meaning, since meaning is only created by the perceiver as the text is read (Bressler 71). What this means in the interpretation of literature is that the individual reader's background experience and consciousness exert considerable influence in how a text is understood. In contrast to the New Critics who warned against subjectivity in reading and believed that an objective, "quasi-scientific" approach was best suited to understanding a text, for reader-response critics, how each reader responds to a text is what provides final meaning. Indeed, the very process of how readers read a text becomes central to reader-response criticism (Guerin et al. 356-357).

Interestingly, reader-response approaches actually include a fairly wide spectrum of adherents in relationship to the primacy of the reader in creating meaning. Perhaps concerned about the relativity of how readers may differ in their responses to a literary text (is every personal reading of a text valid, no matter how bizarre or how distant from textual details?), some reader-response theorists, such as Louise Rosenblatt, emphasize that any single literary text circumscribes possible reader meanings and responses; that is, *not every meaning* is possible from any single text (Guerin et al. 359). Indeed, some theorists go even further and underscore that readers from the same culture or socialization process, given the same practice and experience, will doubtless come to similar conclusions about how they understand any given literary text (Bressler 74). Such a culturally-determined or socially-constructed group of readers is sometimes referred to as an "interpretive community" (Tyson 171).

The reader-response approach has been particularly appealing as a pedagogical tool in secondary classes and beginning college classes. Such techniques as reflective journaling about the assigned reading, the construction of personal visual responses in the form of collages and posters, small group discussions which emphasize readers' initial feelings about texts, and other classroom methods of providing for personal reader reactions—all are related to a desire to instigate reader involvement with a text and provide ways of validating individual responses to literature.[5]

---

[5] See, for example, Nicholas J. Karolides, ed., *Reader Response in Secondary and College Classrooms*, 2nd ed. (Mahwah, NJ: Lawrence Erlbaum Associates, 2000).

Reader-response theory is not inherently antagonistic to the Christian world view. As Michael Vander Weel has pointed out, the Christian tradition has long been interested "in the effects of speech and writing on listeners and readers" (127). Furthermore, reader-response theory has never been monolithic and does not espouse any "single philosophical starting point," but instead has provided a meaningful alternative to theories that overemphasize the importance of the author and/or the dominance of the text (132). As such, it provides a meaningful basis for feminist and cultural criticism as well as the new historicism when the emphasis is on how social interaction within cultures contributes to how readers interpret texts (142-143). Similar insights about how Christian cultures help form reader responses and interpretations can grow out of the Christian application of reader-response theory. On the other hand, Ryken rightly warns Christians about "certain extreme forms of reader-centered criticism" which deny the possibility of authors and texts communicating meaning and stress that readers "create their own meanings in place of the text" (*Windows* 108). Such approaches undercut the important Christian emphasis on God's ability to communicate with human beings in any meaningful and consistent manner.

Psychoanalytic Criticism

Although modern psychological theory as applied to literary texts appears somewhat in Frye's work (see above), it is much more obvious in the writings of critics influenced by Sigmund Freud and his followers. These psychoanalytic critics base their understanding of how to approach a text on the premise that art reveals the unconscious much in the way that dreams do; hence, the psychoanalytical approaches used to uncover the unconscious motives for human behavior when applied to literary texts and their authors can help to reveal meanings not otherwise accessible if readers do not attempt to get beneath and behind the surface language of the text (Bressler 153). The psychological approach is most often employed in two ways: as a means of providing insights into how an author's biographical details and psychological motives are reflected in texts, and as an approach to understanding the psychology of created characters in narrative and dramatic literature. In general, psychoanalytic critics employ standard approaches regarding dream symbolism, sexual obsessions, and developmental phases as outlined in Freudian psychology and its more recent adaptations (see Bressler 149-153 and 159-160). Since Freud himself depended to some extent on his readings of influential literary texts as a means of establishing his models for human behavior (his insights about the

Oedipus complex partially stemmed from his reading and analysis of Sophocles' classic drama *Oedipus Rex)*, the application of psychoanalytic understandings to literature has seemed a particularly rich linkage during the twentieth century. While the psychological approach to literature can result in penetrating insights into the motives of literary characters and the complex relationship of authors' lives to the texts they produce, this approach often does not attempt to address questions of aesthetic form (Guerin et al. 126). But that limitation is somewhat compensated for by the resulting adaptability of the approach as a supplement to other approaches, such as feminism and cultural criticism (Bressler 148).

As Alan Jacobs points out, even though Freudian theory raises serious questions about certain basic traditional Christian views of the nature of the universe and the origins of guilt in human beings, Christian critics and readers, themselves highly influenced by modern psychology, have in general been able to merge these understandings into their traditional belief system without undue discomfort ("Psychological" 94). Indeed, perhaps that merging has been too comfortable. As Jacobs argues, the fact that Freudian psychoanalytical criticism and traditional Christianity represent two widely divergent "teleologies" must result in the Christian psychological critic's taking "a different road […] at precisely the point where their views of the 'nature and destiny of man' diverge […]" (116-117).

Postmodernism/Post-Structuralism

Deconstructionism

The most controversial and revolutionary literary theory to emerge in the latter half of the twentieth century is deconstructionism. Generally attributed to Jacques Derrida, the French thinker, deconstructionism centers on the inadequacies and unreliability of language to communicate meaning. Truth, for deconstruction, is relative, created by the individual and by the social group within which the individual functions.

Derrida's criticism of language centered on the inadequacies of the structuralist linguistic thinking about meaning. Structural linguists had pointed out that words and their meanings are arbitrary, but they had not questioned that meaning exists. As modernists, they rejected "being" as the center of meaning, but they did not reject "knowing" as that center, and they had confidence that language structures existed in all human beings and that those structures and systems work together to provide confidence in humanity's ability to know reliably (Sire 176-184; Jacobs, "Deconstruction" 173-176).

Derrida, however, questioned the reliability of language as a system that provides confidence in meaning. His questions rested on his analysis of "logocentrism," the "Western proclivity" to require some sort of "transcendental" fixed point from which meaning radiates. Derrida attempts to show how those fixed points "invented" by Western thinkers (whether they be *"God, reason, origin, being, essence, truth, humanity, begging, end,* and *self"*) are all only words, examples of language which in itself is unreliable and variable (Bressler 124-125). Language's unreliability he demonstrates by noting that binary oppositions or differences that establish meaning are based on hierarchies of superior over inferior (good is better than bad, true is better than false) and that these hierarchies are, after all, only arbitrary and may have no relation to anything at all as far as eternal or fixed meanings are concerned. Without a fixed center from which to judge differences in meanings, all meanings become relative and ephemeral. Language itself becomes a system that is given to misunderstandings, confusion, and contradictions. Interpretations inevitably fall apart because they are imprisoned in a system whose meanings are never fixed. "Never can we state a text's definitive meaning, for it has none" (Bressler 129). Instead, texts will mean different things to different people and different things to the same person when read again. And communicating one's interpretation of a text inevitably will be incomplete since the language system used for that communication is also incomplete and contradictory. Texts, therefore, tend to fall apart or deconstruct (Tyson 252).

In some ways, of course, deconstruction seems very like reader-response criticism in that both seem to indicate that interpretation depends heavily on the reader. The difference is that reader-response criticism, at least as theorized by Louise Rosenblatt, assumes that language has some sort of reliability for both the text and the reader and even goes so far as to suggest that the text controls or sets parameters on the meanings readers help to create (Vander Weel 140-41). In contrast, deconstructionism emphasizes that language itself is unreliable, that meaning is always fleeting, and, very importantly, that agreement on meanings is really only the product of "ideological readings" imposed upon individuals because of the cultures in which they live (Tyson 252).

A deconstructionist critic's main task in dealing with literary texts is to show where the language of those texts breaks down to reveal "'undecidability'" and to emphasize how "the complex operations" of "ideologies" have affected the text's oppositional language and meanings (Tyson 252). Deconstructionist critics use close readings, similar to the methodological thoroughness of the New Critics, often centering on how individual words or phrases undercut or contradict what seems to be the larger and wrongly-assumed unified meanings of a text (Tyson 252-253).

Deconstructionist theory is the essential lynch-pin of postmodernism in literary criticism. As such, it presents particular problems for the Christian. First, its attack on the real existence of "transcendental" "centers" as being nothing but privileged language constructions can be seen as undercutting Christian confidence in the very existence of God (Jacobs, "Deconstruction" 178-179). Second, its emphasis on the unreliability of language and the variability or relativity of meaning erodes confidence in communicating anything meaningful about reality, including the proclamation of the Christian world view (Jacobs 191). Finally, its emphasis on how ideology alone coerces common understandings of meaning emphasizes how arbitrary power can play an undue role in human existence (Sire 181). Christianity, like any other ideology, is, therefore, merely an example of how power rather than truth can control human meaning.

On the positive side, however, what deconstructionist criticism has provided for the Christian is a reminder of how language by its very nature is given to "difficulties in communication" (Longman III 44). Of course, this emphasis on the difficulties of language is not really news. As Alan Jacobs asserts: "*Of course* words have histories; *of course* meanings are created through habitual usage and general agreement. Each element of any language may be arbitrary at its origin—but we are not at its origin; we are in the middle of a long and complex history of generated meaning and value" ("Deconstruction" 196). To acknowledge the difficulties of language in establishing meaning, however, does not have to result in claiming that texts will always dissolve into meaninglessness or in accepting the deconstructionist theory that power alone is the essential construct in a group's common understandings.

Feminist and Cultural Approaches

The idea of "interpretive communities," key to reader-response theories, and the idea of power as key to controlling group understandings of meaning, basic to deconstructionist theory, are good entry points for the consideration of several such contemporary communities and their approaches to literary texts. In some ways, these approaches to literature are not strictly postmodern in their basic premises. For example, their emphasis on ideology and history, on how literature reveals bias, and on how literature should change society has common elements with the old pre-modern historical and moral criticism. Their willingness to employ close readings of texts to support their interpretations certainly aligns them with the New Criticism and modernism. But their dependence on deconstructionist theory to emphasize the relativity of language and to reveal how societal and cultural groupings control thinking together with their flourishing in the post-1950s decades makes their designation as postmodern appropriate.

Perhaps the most influential "interpretive community" in the United States and Europe has been those women and men who have contributed to the rise of modern feminism. Although certainly not a monolithic movement in that feminists include a reasonably broad spectrum of religious, political, and social opinions, feminism does loosely coalesce around certain perceptions about the treatment of women: that men "have oppressed women," that male-dominated societies have not allowed women a "voice," that the result has "trivialized what it means to be a woman," and that an appropriate "goal is to change this degrading view of women so that [...] each woman is a valuable person possessing the same privileges and rights as every man" (Bressler 180). Feminist literary criticism centers on several important concerns: (1) the need to recognize appropriately the contributions of women writers and their writings, works which have often been ignored or discounted by the dominating male cultures of the past; (2) the need to read literary texts from a feminist perspective, noting how male writers have revealed their inevitable anti-feminist attitudes in the way they have developed their themes and their created women literary characters or how female writers have been limited in their own development of themes and characters by the restrictions placed upon them by their male-dominated societies; (3) and the need to understand how gender inevitably shows itself in the act of creating and writing, thus providing opportunities to understand how male and female perspectives, ways of thinking, and ways of writing are richly embedded in the literary texts they produce (Bressler 190-191).

Other interpretive communities, somewhat marginalized in the same way as women have been, also in recent decades have asserted their own identities as important influences on how literature should be read. Marxist criticism (or economic criticism), for example, stems from the nineteenth-century economic-political-social theories of Karl Marx and Friedrich Engels (Bressler 211), centering on the inevitable class conflicts that emerge in any society in which there are economic divisions based upon who has money (and thus power) and who does not (Tyson 50). As applied to literature, Marxist critics value those texts which give appropriate attention to the plights of the lower classes and show sympathy for common people, but such critics react strongly against those texts and writers who apparently support capitalism's inherent approval of economic class distinctions. Those texts which show an awareness of the need for social/political change are those praised by Marxist critics, while those that seem comfortable with the status quo of Western society or which ignore the social problems of class and economic divisions cannot receive approval by the Marxist interpretive community (Tyson 65). Marxist critics first flourished in the United States during the Great Depression of the 1930s when it seemed relatively clear that capitalism was failing and that social change was necessary. After World War II, with the distinct cold war conflict between Western capitalism and institutionalized Marxism in the form of the so-called Iron-Curtain and Bamboo-Curtain nations, Marxist criticism declined in influence in the United States, although leftist critics continued their pronounced class-conscious perspectives in scholarly and critical circles in Europe and the United States (Bressler 210-211). Even though institutionalized communism suffered an almost lethal blow with the democratization of Russia and its satellite countries in Europe in the late 1980s and early 1990s, Marxist-influenced criticism continues to be an important literary perspective today for it provides for its adherents "a meaningful way to understand history and current events" (Tyson 49) and a means to value literature that criticizes the flaws of capitalism (Tyson 65-66).

Some interpretive communities are united by such issues as race or sexual orientation rather than by gender or economic-political theory. Postcolonial and African-American criticism, for example, approach literature with an eye to how people of color have in the past been overlooked as writers of worthy texts or have been portrayed in biased and marginalized ways by the dominating white cultures (Bressler 268-270). In the United States, there is a growing movement to emphasize how "Latina/o," American Indian, and Asian-American writers and texts have been similarly overlooked in literary studies of the past (Geurin et al. 260-270). Finally, Lesbian, Gay, and Queer Criticism has become important in theoretical circles in the United States during the past three decades, providing an opportunity to recognize how writers who are homosexual and/or who explore homoerotic themes, however hidden, have been ignored or condemned because of society's prejudices (Tyson 317-323).

All of these interpretive communities share certain characteristics: marginalization because of gender, race, sexual orientation, or political attitudes. Their common core is the desire to become recognized as important and valid contributors to society and to literature. In one way or another, each group points out the flaws of society or the power system that controls society and calls for social-political-economic change. Indeed, their recognition that power plays significant roles in how people lead their lives and that power, thus, inevitably controls to some extent how literary texts are approached or valued is, perhaps, the most influential contribution to literary studies which these interpretive communities have provided.

Of particular difficulty to Christians is the reality that institutionalized Christianity has been a main target of these interpretive communities for its seeming support of their marginalization. Marxists have been very forthright in their criticism which finds traditional religion and, in particular, Christianity, blameworthy for its seeming institutionalization of class differences and its resistance to social improvement (Tyson 56). Traditional Christianity, however, has also been criticized for its racial, colonial, sexual, and gender prejudices and for its slowness in coming to grips with its seemingly "church-approved" mistreatment of powerless groups (Ryken, "Afterword" 294-297). The challenge for Christians is to admit the validity of some of these charges while at the same time remaining loyal to a belief system that places God at the center of the universe with a plan of salvation that responds to social and political needs, even if that response has too often been ignored or de-emphasized by Christians in the past.

The New Historicism

In important ways, the so-called new historicist approach to understanding literary texts, influenced directly by the ideas of Michel Foucault, attempts to address issues of power as a main component of the literary process while at the same time grounding this examination of power in non-traditional, but defendable, explorations of history and culture (Bressler 241-243). The new historicists cast a much wider net in their connection of the historical and cultural milieu to literature than did the "old" historical literary critics and scholars of the past. Indeed, the new historicists, influenced by reading theory and by postmodernism and deconstructionism, believe that only the most basic "facts" can be established by the supposedly objective approach to history, fundamental to former historical/critical understandings of literature. Instead, they emphasize that all examinations of the past are colored by the historical interpreter and the culture and culture's language within which the interpreter works. Thus, their main interest in history really centers in their interest in interpretation and how interpretation has influenced literary production and reception throughout the ages (Tyson 278-279). Basic to such an understanding of the historical process is the idea that the various complex interactions of power in culture inevitably shape writers as they write and readers as they read. Uncovering the complex historical power interactions that affect writing and the interpretation of writing is the basic purpose of a new historicist approach to literature (Tyson 280-281).

Traditional historical approaches to literature often emphasize how philosophical movements or dominant world views are revealed in literary texts while new historicists search out unexpected connections inherent in the cultural system surrounding text production and reading (Guerin et al. 250). Since they see all of history as a complex series of interactions and interpretations, the new historicists are able to find surprising links between what at first seem widely divergent historical phenomena. Charles Bressler, for example, notes that new historicism might connect "Sophia Hawthorne's having a headache after reading *The Scarlet Letter*" to the happy "ending of [...] *The House of Seven Gables*" or "the climate and environs of Elmira, New York" to "some locations, descriptions, and actions in Mark Twain's *Huckleberry Finn*" (246).

As with feminism and the various cultural approaches to literature discussed earlier, new historicism, with its emphasis upon power interactions within society and how those interactions affect text production and the reading of texts, inevitably can reveal the repressive tendencies of established Christianity in past and present Western culture and how these traits have negatively influenced literature and its reception. As such, new historicism presents a challenge to the Christian believer who must sort through the often justified insights into religious abuses of power without losing faith in the Christian world view. John D. Cox argues that Christians must reject the new historicist position that assumes "that the truth about human history consists of nothing more than mutual predation" and must continue to view history, even though characterized by "power, greed, lust, envy and conspicuous consumption," as "the scene of God's redemptive drama" (262, 264).

Issues of the Canon

Of particular importance during the postmodern era has been the controversy over what literary works should be a part of the so-called literary canon. Which works deserve to be read? What works should be considered a part of great literature? What texts should be taught in the schools?

The *Oxford English Dictionary* defines "canon" as "any collection or list of books of the Bible accepted by the Christian Church as genuine or inspired" or "any set of sacred books." The word itself comes from the Latin term having to do with "measuring line" or "rule" (see the *American Heritage Dictionary*). For the Christian, of course, the canon refers to the various texts that make up the Bible—that is, those books that meet the tests or measuring lines established by the Christian Church during the past two thousand years (Cowan and Guinness 25). During the nineteenth century, as the influence of Christianity waned, literary critics began to advance the notion that art and literature might become a viable substitute for religion in helping humans to live in the best way possible. Critics, such as Matthew Arnold, emphasized that people should read the great texts. Such texts became thought of as a kind of "'secular scripture'" (Cowan and Guinness 25-26). But, of course, such lists of texts were constructed by the dominating power groups of the time—critics, scholars, intellectuals, teachers—most of whom were male, in England and America, white, and, at least nominally, Christian.

What feminism, cultural criticism, and new historicism have centered on is the inadequacy of this traditional literary canon because of its exclusion of texts written by women, by people of certain racial or powerless groups, or by people whose political opinions attack the traditional power groups that control the canon. Deconstruction has added the further ingredient of questioning any text's superiority over another text—the basic premise on which any canon of texts exists—since meaning is constantly in flux and value judgments are merely reflections of the moment as formed by individual responses and/or by the controlling power structures of a given society.

In the United States, the battles over what texts should be read reached their height in the late 1980s and the early 1990s with the publication of such books as Allan Bloom's *The Closing of the American Mind* and E.D. Hirsch's *Cultural Literacy: What Every American Needs to Know* as well as the highly-publicized controversies over what required courses at leading universities were including on their reading lists.[6] Both Bloom and Hirsch attacked the growing willingness of so-called "liberal" groups of feminist and cultural critics and teachers who had pointedly criticized the established literary canon for its exclusion of works not deemed acceptable to

---

[6] A good, brief summary of and reaction to the canon controversy can be found in John Searle, "The Storm over the University," *Falling into Theory: Conflicting Views on Reading Literature*, ed. David H. Richter (Boston: Bedford Books of St. Martin's Press, 1994), 79-88.

the white male establishment of the past. Both books emphasized the importance of the Western classics as a means of imparting sound humanistic values long central to Western culture. Similarly, newspaper accounts of the faculty battles over what should be read at universities in required general education courses have painted a dire picture of what is happening to American culture as a result of the opening up of the canon.

There is no doubt that the concerns raised by the critics of the so-called established canon have made a difference in reading choices within the schools of the United States. In many ways, the publishers of textbooks and anthologies for the schools are the transmitters of the canon, with the editors of those same books being the arbiters of taste for the vast audience of readers enrolled in secondary schools and colleges (Richter, *Falling* 112). When I compare the anthology I first used as a student in an American Literature course in 1959 at Pacific Union College (*American Poetry and Prose* produced under the general editorial control of Norman Foerster, the important early booster of American Literature as a respectable academic and scholarly discipline) to the present anthology I use for the course in American Literature I regularly teach at Andrews University (*The Norton Anthology of American Literature*, edited by N. Baym et al., with Baym being one of the leading feminist scholars in literary circles in the United States), I can easily notice the difference in the canon that each anthology represents. The Foerster collection begins with materials from John Smith and William Bradford, respectively—leaders, as well as writers about, the Jamestown and Plymouth colonies. No Native American writers are included, and few African-American writers were deemed important enough to be represented. Prior to the turn of the twentieth century, only four women are represented. In contrast, the Norton collection begins with non-English writing in translation from European explorers and settlers in the Caribbean and Central America (people such as Columbus), includes a number of Native American materials throughout the centuries, and features a variety of African-American writers from the eighteenth century up to the present. Women writers prior to and throughout the twentieth century are also well represented, as are modern Latino and Asian-American writers. Finally, the sexual orientations of writers in the Norton collection are regularly noted. The introduction to Walt Whitman, for example, in the old Foerster anthology, labels Whitman's homosexuality only in a brief negative comment as "an abnormal attraction" to men (846), whereas the Norton anthology, issued forty years later, explores in some detail and without prejudice how Whitman's poetry reveals his sexual orientation (1002-1004).

Conservative Christians (oftentimes also conservative in their social and political views) have generally expressed concern about the opening up of the literary canon. While Christians can applaud the need to welcome "neglected writers and traditions" (Cowan and Guiness 16-17), they also express concern that "the canon is under attack by critics who are skeptical of the veneration and meaning that generations of readers have attached to what is loosely called the great tradition" (Ryken, "Afterword" 297). A main reason for some lack of comfort with the opening of the canon is that the critical theorists who champion that opening are themselves somewhat hostile to Christianity and its traditions. Leland Ryken, for example, notes that such leading critical theorists as Jonathan Culler and J. Hillis Miller in the United States have either attacked or pointedly disregarded Christian contributions to literary traditions and theory (295-296). Given the obvious truth that the vast majority of Western writers during the past two thousand years have been Christian, such critical reactions seem misplaced.

Conservative Christians are not the only ones bothered by political and social attacks on the traditional Western canon, however. Even a non-Christian critic like Harold Bloom raises important reservations about the erosion of regard for the Western classics. Bloom's grounds are not religious, however, but aesthetic. In *The Western Canon: The Books and School of the Ages*, Bloom asserts that "academic Marxism, Feminism, and New Historicism" are misguided in their attempt to see a work of literature as "primarily a social document" (18). Says Bloom,

> If we read the Western Canon in order to form our social, political, or personal moral values, I firmly believe we will become monsters of selfishness and exploitation. To read in the service of any ideology is not, in my judgment, to read at all. [...] All that the Western Canon can bring one is the proper use of one's own solitude, that solitude whose final form is one's confrontation with one's own mortality. (29-30)

Bloom goes ahead to assert that "canons always do indirectly serve the social and political, and indeed the spiritual, concerns and aims of the wealthier classes of each generation of Western society" (33). However, those issues should never be paramount in deciding what one reads. Instead, what the classics rest on is their "aesthetic power" and "aesthetic dignity" (36). What makes a work canonical for Bloom is its "strangeness, a mode of originality that either cannot be assimilated, or that so assimilates us that we cease to see it as strange.[...] When you read a canonical work for a first time you encounter a stranger, an uncanny startlement rather than a fulfillment of expectations" (3).

The recent battles over what should be read illustrate vividly something often forgotten by the leading proponents of change in the canon as well as by those (often conservative Christians) who want to hold onto the "old" canon as if it represented some sort of eternal life preserver—that is, that the literary canon has never been fixed and permanent, that there has always been a shifting of tastes and values in Western societies, and that these tastes and values inevitably produce variations in what is included for reading in, for example, literature anthologies and courses. As Bloom notes, "as no secular canon is ever closed, what is now acclaimed as 'opening up the canon' is a strictly redundant operation" (37).

An interesting Christian reaction to the changing canon is a work edited by Louise Cowan and Os Guinness, entitled *Invitation to the Classics: A Guide to Books You've Always Wanted to Read*, an openly Christian text which attempts to point out the difference between the secular literary canon, with its works which "go in and out of fashion," as opposed to the classics—that is, works which "endure from age to age" (26). According to Cowan and Guinness,

> It is inconceivable that at any time in the future Homer's *Odyssey*, Dante's *Divine Comedy*, or the tragedies of Shakespeare will fall completely out of favor [...] . They are too much a part of history ever to be removed. The role of the classics in the formation of modern culture is so foundational that in a very real sense, we know the classics before we read them. Their values, visions, stories, and metaphors have shaped our culture and our self-understanding in myriad ways that are undeniable but impossible to quantify. (26-27)

The works discussed in Cowan and Guinness are those deemed to possess lasting qualities which can provide a means "to help reawaken Western people to the vibrant heritage of these classics that are rich in themselves and in their two-thousand-year relationship to the Christian faith" (13). Although the approach by Cowan and Guinness rightly emphasizes how selected works of the past and present show particular affinity to Christian ideals and values, it ignores the rich contributions of writers who do not fit easily into the Christian world view. And, of course, calling their selected works "classics" does not really diffuse the central issues raised in the controversy over the canon but merely substitutes their own version of a Christian literary canon in place of a more "secular" reading list.

CHAPTER THREE
CHRISTIANITY AND LITERATURE

For close to two thousand years, Western culture has itself been dominated by the Christian faith. Attempts to make clear the function of art in
Western experience have, therefore, up until recent times, been essentially Christian
in their basic premises. In the last couple of centuries, however, as Christian
beliefs and traditions have been questioned and criticized, the separation between Christian approaches to the arts and "secular" approaches has become
more and more distinct. As Ryken notes: "Until recently, it was possible for
Christian criticism to merge its identity with the critical establishment. [...]
Today, however, a cozy alliance between Christian criticism and the larger critical establishment is not an option. With no critical establishment on which to
piggyback, Christian critics have no alternative but to establish their own identity" ("Afterword" 297-298). It is essential, therefore, for Christians to assess
again why they read literature and how best to approach the reading of literature.

Traditional Christian Concerns about Literature and the Arts

Of course, somewhat standing in the way of an enriching Christian approach to literature is the traditional Christian antagonism towards the arts
and literature. That antagonism centers on several related concerns: (1) that
as products of the imagination the arts are false and escapist, (2) that the
arts are often corrupting and immoral, and (3) that, if not immoral, the arts
are essentially useless and irrelevant to the spiritual life.

Actually, the view of the arts as false to reality appears first in Western
culture not during the Christian period but rather in the so-called pagan Greek
and Roman cultures. Plato is the most eloquent spokesman for this position.
According to Plato, truth exists in the eternal forms or "transcendental Ideas,"
of which the external world is but an imitation. Imaginative writers imitate
the external world which is already an imitation. Therefore, the poet is "'thrice
removed from the truth'" and can easily mislead or misapprehend truth with
consequential effects upon the reader (Ryken, *Triumphs* 14).

Often linked to the concern about the essential falsehood of the arts are the views that art is corrupting or immoral and that the arts are useless, especially to the Christian life. Reciting the list of Christian critics of art is certainly intimidating: Tertullian, who believed that the arts were demonic and were intended "'to turn man from the Lord'"; Augustine, who after his conversion condemned literature for teaching "'vice'" and who regretted his own classical education because it had "'forced'" him "'to go astray in the footsteps of these poetic fictions'"; and the Puritans of England and America who lashed out against fictionalized stories and the theater, perhaps best represented by the words of Richard Baxter who claimed that such endeavors "'dangerously bewitcheth and corrupteth the minds of the young and empty people'" and result in wasting "'precious time in which much better work might be done'" (Ryken, *Triumphs* 14-16). Even in the twentieth century, as Ryken notes, Christian critics still have attacked the arts and literature, especially novels and dramas, and wondered whether Christian students should take "a course in writing poetry and fiction when the time might be spent on something allegedly more useful" (17).

The Biblical Basis for a Christian Approach to Literature

To some extent, postmodernism opens up the door to a Christian literary approach in a way that modernism never did. Since a basic premise of postmodernism is its emphasis on how scientific rationalism (the impetus behind modernism) is merely an interpretation of reality constructed by a power group and is of itself no better than any other power group's search for meaning, the Christian is suddenly placed on somewhat "even" ground in asserting Christian faith as a foundation for understanding the place of the arts. Since there are a number of power groups jockeying for position in relationship to how literature should be read (see Chapter Two), why not a Christian literary criticism to take its place along with the others as a viable method of understanding texts? Yet, even while asserting such privilege, Christianity is somewhat on the defensive since the very postmodernist criticism which allows for a variety of political, cultural, gender, and sexual approaches to literature also is severely critical of Christian attitudes and beliefs as representative of a dominant religious culture of the past that has excluded the very groups now agitating for inclusion (Ryken, "Afterword" 295-297).

Where, then, does the Christian critic and reader begin when attempting to establish a Christian approach to literature? Ryken emphasizes that such an approach must start with "the acceptance of Christian doctrine and morality (both ultimately derived from the Bible)" and combine that "authoritative framework" with a willingness to link "Christian truth" with "literature or literary theory" ("Afterword" 298).

Since the Bible is the basis for Christian faith, the Scriptures must be the starting point for a Christian approach to literature. But where in the Bible does one go in order to find materials to undergird a Christian view of the arts? Two important biblical principles have proved fundamentally significant in explanations of why the arts and literature are crucial to the Christian life: (1) the doctrine of creation and (2) the fact that the preponderance of material in the Bible is itself in the form of literature.

Creating in the Image of God

Perhaps the most carefully developed Christian view of how the biblical doctrine of creation becomes a blueprint for human creation in the arts is developed by Dorothy Sayers, the British medievalist and detective-story writer, in her essay on "The Image of God," collected as part of *Christian Letters to a Post-Christian World* (100-106). Sayers bases her view on her analysis of the creation stories in Genesis. Reiterated throughout the first chapter of Genesis is God's creative power. Note the first text in the Bible, Genesis 1:1: "In the beginning God *created* the heaven and the earth" (italics added for emphasis). The rest of the chapter recounts God's creative activities throughout those seven days: air, water, light, grass, flowers, trees, birds, fish, animals, followed by the creation of man and woman. "And God said, Let us make man in our image, after our likeness. So God created man in his own image, in the image of God created he him; male and female created he them" (Genesis 1:26-27).

But how are man and woman like God, asks Sayers. How are we made in His image? Sayers emphasizes that no detailed information about God is provided in the first chapter of Genesis except for specifics about His creative power. She concludes, therefore, that human beings are most like God in having "the desire and the ability to make things" (100-101). But, of course, this creative bent in men and women is not on the same level as God's creative power. We cannot create something from nothing as He does in Genesis 1. "We can," in Sayers's words, "only rearrange the unalterable and indestructible units of matter in the universe and build them into new forms" (103). Anything that human beings make in whatever arena of life images God's creativity, but those things which humans create in the arts are most like God's creation out of nothing (although, of course, not quite the same) in that they are products of the imagination, as His creation was such a product, and "not simply a rearrangement of matter" (105). "This experience of the creative imagination in the common man or woman and in the artists is the only thing we have to go upon in entertaining and formulating the concept of creation. Outside our own experience of procreation and creation we can form no notion of how anything comes into being" (105). Sayers goes ahead, then, to raise poets to the level of importance of theologians for Christians in understanding the central Christian truth about God's creativity and its relationship to the human creative process (105-106). As Ryken notes, "To delight in the work of human imagination is to value the image of God in people, and to write imaginative literature is to express that image" (*Triumphs* 40).

One cannot ignore, however, the historical discomfort of Christianity with the imagination and its products. Ryken emphasizes how the creation story reveals God as the greatest of all imaginers, thus providing Christians with "a more convincing reason for relishing the imagination than the world at large may have" (*Windows* 57). Christians, however, have often equated the imagination with mere fantasy, fabrication, or lies. Certainly, modern Christians, perhaps influenced unduly by scientific rationalism, tend to distrust "the power of metaphor or paint on canvas or music to express the truth," preferring "theological abstraction and outline" to "the imaginative boldness of the writers of the Bible" (58). The Bible as a work of imaginative power provides the second important starting place for a Christian theory of literature.

The Bible and Literature

God's creating character and its imaging in human creativity can perhaps be best explained to Christians who are antagonistic to the arts by emphasizing how important literature is to the very Scriptures that guide Christian life. Bible writers, moved by God, wrote their works in literary forms which are typical products of the human imagination. Ryken emphasizes that "there is no trace in the Bible of a negative attitude toward literature" (*Triumphs* 21). He contrasts this to the "Platonic antipathy to literature" (22). Jesus used imaginative approaches to enthrall his audience. He told stories and spoke in figures (*Windows* 58). Large portions of the Scriptures are narrative or poetic in form and not "an expository treatise on systematic theology [...]" (*Triumphs* 22). Like all literature, therefore, "the Bible is experiential and concrete" and is rich in its varieties of artistic literary forms embraced by its writers, "including narrative or story, epic, tragedy, satire, lyric poetry, epithalamium, elegy, encomium, proverb, parable, pastoral, prophecy, gospel, epistle, oratory and apocalypse" (22). Because literature is so crucial to the Bible, Christians must be very careful when they talk about the unimportance of literature.

A Christian Approach to Literature

Given the importance of the doctrine of creation and the centrality of the Scriptures to the Christian life and the crucial intertwining of both to literature, what are the central concerns that should characterize a Christian approach to literature? Three important foundational premises—all linked to God's creating character—emerge as significant building blocks: (1) the importance of beauty in creation; (2) the emphasis on pleasure as an appropriate aspect of human experience; and (3) the place of truth in the development of Christian character.

The Place of Beauty in Christian Experience

God, the Great Imaginer, created a world of beauty. Ellen White writes: "As it came from the Creator's hand, not only the Garden of Eden but the whole earth was exceedingly beautiful" (*Education* 22). Thousands of years after that creation, even in a world marred by sin and corruption, human beings still enjoy the glories of nature. They drive hundreds and thousands of miles to view snow-capped mountains, rugged coastlines, crystalline lakes, gigantic trees, even parched deserts and rugged canyons.

While Christians have little trouble admiring the beauties of God's creation in nature, they sometimes have difficulty appreciating the beauty of what people, made in the image God, themselves create. Ryken notes that James 1:17 tells us that "'every good endowment and every perfect gift is from above, coming down from the Father of lights.'" Beauty in literature and the arts is also from God, he suggests, and, as such, becomes an appropriate avenue for Christian appreciation of God's character (*Windows* 74). One of the troubling characteristics of recent postmodern approaches to literature has been the tendency to dismiss beauty as irrelevant to an evaluation of the worth of a text and, instead, to emphasize the political or social issues raised by a text as primary areas of interest. A Christian approach to literature, however, recognizes the God-given example of created beauty and embraces an approach that attempts to reveal such beauty through aesthetic and textual analysis (Ryken, "Afterword" 299).

Pleasure as a Meaningful Element in Christian Experience

Closely related to a Christian emphasis on beauty in creation and the arts is the corollary principle that pleasure is an appropriate and necessary aspect of Christian life. Surely the appropriateness of enjoyment is central to the creation story in Genesis 1 when again and again God responds to His own creating activities with the following words: "And God saw that it was good." Ryken notes that pleasure is "one of the recurrent themes in the Psalms" (*Windows* 75). In the New Testament, Paul writes the following to Timothy: "Charge them that are rich in this world, that they be not highminded, nor trust in uncertain riches, but in the living God, who giveth us richly all things to enjoy" (1 Tim. 6:17, KJV). Ryken emphasizes how this passage establishes "three important principles: (1) God is the giver of all good things, (2) He gives people these things to enjoy, and (3) the misuse of them consists not in enjoyment of them but in trusting them or making idols of them" (76). Literary beauty can provide pleasure for the Christian reader, a pleasure that is of itself a God-endorsed activity as evidenced in the responses of people over the ages to the aesthetic beauty and pleasure resultant from reading the Bible.

But both beauty and pleasure as experienced by the Christian reader carry with them the inherent qualities of all human experience since the fall—the elements of corruption and evil that taint not only the arts but all people, all of nature, indeed all of God's creation. As Ryken suggests, "beauty and pleasure can be used in evil and destructive ways" (*Windows* 77). It is this concern about corruption, evil, and sin which makes the Christian experience fraught with difficulties and leads to a consideration of the third element that must undergird a Christian approach to literature—the question of truth in the arts.

Truth in the Arts and Literature

As important as beauty and pleasure are to a Christian approach to literature, questions of truth or meaning loom even larger. All literature is the product of the artful use of language. In contrast to postmodern theorists who have questioned the possibility of communicating meaning in language, Christian readers must insist that language is a God-ordained method of communicating, essential to spiritual growth and meaningful human interaction (Vande Kopple 200-201). As John 1:1 underscores: "In the beginning was the Word" (KJV). Even though language is fraught with complexities and ambiguities, resulting in human misunderstandings and confusion, Christian readers of literature affirm that texts can and do communicate meanings and that these meanings conform to the general parameters set up by an author's intention, by a text's wording, and by readers' backgrounds and experiences (Ryken, *Windows* 108, 125-128).

It is important to consider just what kinds of meanings or truth texts communicate. A good starting place for the Christian reader is the larger consideration of where truth originates. As Arthur Holmes asserts, God as

> the all-wise Creator of all [...] has perfect knowledge of everything we ever sought to know or do. The truth about the physical order is known perfectly to him, the truth about humankind and society, and the truth about everything we ever wondered about in our most perplexed moments. The early church fathers summed this up in what has become a guidepost for Christian scholars ever since—*all truth is God's truth, wherever it be found.* (17)

As a result, all areas of experience, "the worlds of literature, philosophy, history, science, and art become the Christian's rightful domain" (17).

But even though all real and lasting truth comes from God and all lasting meaning for the Christian is centered in God, not everything in life is truthful. The Christian doctrine of the fall of humanity emphasizes how evil has tainted the world and how falsehood affects all of human experience. In spite of this post-Eden condition, however, "truth shows up all over the place, fragmentarily perhaps and with pervasive misinterpretation, and God the Creator is ultimately the source of all that is true" (Holmes 17).

When dealing with the content or meaning of literature, then, the Christian must do what the Christian does with all aspects of human experience—make judgments as to what is true or valuable as opposed to that which is not. As T. S. Eliot emphasizes as the basic premise of his essay "Religion and Literature": "Literary criticism should be completed by criticism from a definite ethical and theological standpoint. [...] In ages like our own [...] it is the more necessary for Christian readers to scrutinize their reading, especially of works of imagination, with explicit ethical and theological standards" (21).

But making Christian judgments about truth and meaning in literature is no easy task. Complexities abound. One way of wrestling with the complexities is to consider the types of truth which literature communicates. It is all too easy to equate truth with events or facts which can be substantiated by observation and evidence. Such a view of truth is highly rationalistic and very dependent upon the influence of modern science and its history of testing hypotheses by rigorous methods and standards. Since the arts are creations of the imagination, however, truth and meaning in literature necessarily include more than just the propositional truth of scientific rationalism. Literature is also not history—that is, it makes no claim to creating a strictly factual account of things that have happened or of events that can be verified by the strict rules of historical investigation. This is not to say that literature cannot include rational propositions or historical facts; it is only to underscore that literature is more than these aspects of experience; hence, discussions of truth and meaning in literature must be more inclusive than Christians have often allowed them to be.

By their very nature, the arts, as products of the imagination, even though they are based in empirical reality, construct a made-up or created world that is different from the world we experience every day. As such, the arts are indeed fictional and should be discussed by Christians as such. But it is a mistake for Christians to see fiction as the opposite of truth. Instead, fiction should be seen as the opposite of fact. Truth, moreover, for the Christian is not merely the recital of facts that are a part of the empirical world of reality. Truth for the Christian resides in the larger purposes of God and the universe—purposes that are realized only partially through human reason—purposes that may be realized more fully through the processes of the imagination.

Basic to a Christian understanding of literature is this seemingly paradoxical nature of literature—that is, imaginative, "made-up" creations which, although fictional, still at the same time reveal truth. It is what Ryken calls "The 'Lie' That Tells the Truth" (*Windows* 37). Ryken distinguishes three types of truth in his discussion of literature and truth: (1) "Truth about Human Values," (2) "Truthfulness to Reality and Human Experience," and (3) "The Level of Ideas and Philosophy of Life" (29-31). First, since literature is an imaginary revelation of human experience, inevitably it speaks to readers about what writers value in life and "what is *important* in human experience. If you want to know the truth about rock-bottom human nature [...] literature is probably your best source" (29-30). Second, however, in order for its revelation of human values to be credible, literature must be convincing in its evocation of human experience. As such, literature must be based in reality and have a degree of "*representational truth*" or concreteness associated with the world that humans regularly experience (30, 51). Finally, literature not only presents created human experience; it also attempts to provide an "*interpretation*" of that experience as "filtered through the writer's bias" (30). These interpretations inevitably call upon the reader to react on the level of ideas or philosophy of life in an attempt to measure the interpretations of experience provided by the writer against the reader's own value system and world view.

Making Christian Judgments about Literature

The Christian reader, then, judges the truth of a literary text in relationship to its revelation of human values, its representation of human reality, and its interpretation of human experience. Christians compare these aspects of a text with their own Christian view of reality to determine the worth and value of a work of literature. In doing so, however, they will inevitably be faced with further questions and complexities. How should a Christian reader respond to works which are apparently silent regarding Christian values and perspectives? Can a Christian value a work of literature which explicitly contradicts the Christian world view? Should a Christian only read works which are explicitly Christian in their outlook?

One way of attempting to answer these questions is to arbitrarily divide literature into three categories: (1) literature that is "*exclusively Christian*" (Ryken, *Triumphs* 163); (2) literature that is "*inclusively Christian*" (159); and (3) literature that is antagonistic to the Christian world view and Christian morality.[7]

Exclusively Christian Literature

Perhaps the easiest category of literature for the Christian to value is that group of works which show "*viewpoints that are exclusively Christian*" (Ryken, *Triumphs* 163). Such works clearly show conformity to a Christian world view and may be explicitly about elements basic to Christian belief and doctrines or, in a larger way, may present "a Christian slant on whatever topic" treated (163). Standard examples of such works include Dante's *Divine Comedy*, Milton's *Paradise Lost*, Bunyan's *Pilgrim's Progress*, and the religious poetry of John Donne or Gerard Manley Hopkins. Ryken notes that "whenever a work of literature or a given writer's corpus of works elevates God to a position of supremacy and relates all other areas of life to God, it can be identified as possessing a Christian world view" (164).

---

[7]Inevitably, such a division into categories oversimplifies what is in reality a continuum. Also, when looking at any particular work of literature with these categories in mind, one may well find that parts of the work may exhibit some features of one category and other parts may reveal another category.

Works of literature written from a Christian viewpoint do not always immediately reveal themselves as exclusively Christian, however. Although Flannery O'Connor, for example, subscribed to a Christian world view and explicitly announced that her intention in her fiction was to awaken modern readers to their need of Christian faith, readers of her stories sometimes have difficulty accepting the essentially Christian world view the stories project because they are misled by the bizarre and violent events of the narratives themselves. What this suggests is that even with exclusively Christian materials the Christian reader often must analyze carefully in order to reach valid conclusions.

Inclusively Christian Literature

A much larger category is that literature which reveals "*values or viewpoints that are inclusively Christian*" (Ryken, *Triumphs* 159). Even though Western culture was dominated by Christian thinking up until the last two centuries and even though most writers of Western literature during this period of Christian dominance were themselves Christians, what they wrote most often reveals an inclusive rather than an exclusive Christian outlook. Such works reveal viewpoints and ideas that are "not the exclusive property of Christian belief" but instead show human experience through lenses that overlap with those of "other religious and or ethical viewpoints" (159). Examples include lyric poetry which celebrates nature or love without contradicting Christian values; fiction which projects the dismal realities of modern life, thus coinciding with the Christian view of a fallen sinful world; or works which protest social and political conditions and which call for humanity to improve the way people lead their lives (160-61).

Literature in this category may be written by authors who are not believing Christians, as many modern authors are not, even if they are writing within the Western tradition. The fact that non-Christians are the writers does not negate the possibility that their works are inclusively Christian. Ryken cites the "doctrine of common grace" as evidence "that God endows all people, believers and unbelievers alike, with some good qualities and with his natural blessings" (Ryken, *Triumphs* 161). He emphasizes how Christ recognized that sinners may do good (see Luke 6:33) and how Paul noted that "unbelievers have the capacity, *part of the time*, to 'do by nature what the law requires,…even though they do not have the law. They show that what the law requires is written in their hearts'" (Rom. 2:14-15)" (162).

When evaluating works that are inclusively Christian, the Christian reader must be open to valuing works which do not emphasize God or Christ or, for example, the traditional Christian views about the need of repentance, the atonement for sins, or eternal life for the redeemed. Instead, the works, generally silent on explicit Christian concerns, reveal a morality that does not contradict Christian morality but shows those elements of human concern and existence that one might best label as good citizenship. As such, these works of literature must be treated in the same manner that most of human existence is treated whether it be the world of work in a workplace that is not exclusively Christian or the world of leisure in which pleasures and entertainments are not exclusively Christian. The Christian rejoices in and values those elements of these worlds which overlap with Christian morality and perspectives, realizing that, as such, they are revelations of God's continuing love and creatorship.

Works of Literature Antagonistic to Christianity and the Christian World View

From a Christian viewpoint, the most difficult category of works to value are those which are explicitly contrary to Christian perspectives and morality. Many modern writers do not subscribe to Christian beliefs and have adopted philosophical views that run contrary to the Christian faith. Such works may openly attack Christian beliefs and concepts, for example, by positing a world that has no Creator or no God, by emphasizing that human life is accidental in its origin or purposeless in its intent, or by glorifying immoralities such as adultery, murder, lying, and cheating. What is the Christian reader to do with such works?

One possible approach to this problem would be to categorically condemn such texts and to establish lists of "forbidden works" based on their handling of explicit sex or violence or their un-Christian use of explicit language. To do so, however, would mean that Christians are turning their backs on most of modern culture and retreating to some sort of distant nineteenth-century island, unwilling to deal effectively with the contemporary issues and society around them. Such a retreat is neither practical or defensible when one remembers Christ's counsel that His followers are to be "the light of the world" (Matt. 5:14 KJV). One rationale for the Christian reading of modern literature, for example, is the need "of keeping abreast of our own culture" (Ryken, *Triumphs* 176). Such reading should lead Christians "to a sympathetic understanding of non-Christians" (191).

Instead, what the adult Christian is obligated to do is to read carefully selected modern texts in relationship to the Christian world view and to make judgments regarding their truth and meaning, deciding what works have enough value in them to be included as reading for Christian reading and what texts must be discarded as not being appropriately helpful to Christian experience. Ryken lists four questions the Christian can ask in relationship to the reading of modern realistic literature:

1. Does my reading of this work lead me to immoral thoughts or actions?
2. Does the moral depravity that this work portrays call my attention to something about reality that I need to know?
3. Does the overall moral or social significance of this work exceed in importance the offensiveness of some of its parts? Can I minimize the impact of these parts in order to appropriate the larger insights of the work?
4. If I do not enjoy reading this work, is there a reason why I should read it anyway? (*Triumphs* 188-89)

The Christian Approach to Literature as Related to Other Critical Approaches

The Christian approach to literature has much in common with those literary approaches that emphasize content as key in valuing works of literature. As with Feminism, Marxism, and the various cultural approaches, the reader evaluates a work in relationship to the way the content or meaning of a work reveals ideology and perspective and how that ideology and perspective relate to the guiding principles of the relevant interpretive community, in this case Christianity. More importantly, a modern Christian approach really is an extension of the old pre-modern moral criticism (see Chapter Two) which flourished in Western society when Christianity was still a dominant force in critical and academic circles and, thus, brought a Christian world view to its insights into literary works, emphasizing how texts communicated important moral (and at the same time Christian) values. Even as Christianity became widely questioned as a belief system, such a moral critic and writer as Matthew Arnold retained the elements of Christian morality as the basis for his elevation of literature and art to a position of replacements for religion (Ryken, *Triumphs* 73-74).

In contrast to some recent critical approaches which have found little purpose in examining the aesthetic aspects of literature, however, one important quality that a Christian approach to literature recognizes, even with works that are antagonistic to Christian perspectives and morality, is the premise that such works can be valued for their artistic and aesthetic qualities, regardless of their content (Ryken, "Afterword" 299). The Christian can praise the beauty of a text because of its effective use of artistic language and literary devices even though its content may contradict the Christian world view and values. As Ryken observes, "If God is the source of all beauty and artistry, then the artistic dimension of literature is the point at which Christian readers can be unreserved in their enthusiasm for works of non-Christian writers" (*Triumphs* 69). Because formalism or the New Criticism provides an approach that attempts to reveal the aesthetic elements in a text, Christian readers can profitably employ its techniques as they analyze texts in relationship to beauty (Ryken, "Formalism" 15-16).

In the end, then, a Christian approach to literature cannot be seen as totally separate from other approaches. "It cannot avoid being influenced by other theories, nor should it attempt to avoid such influence" ("Afterword" 299). Even those postmodern theories of reading which seem clearly contradictory to the Christian world view can provide meaningful ways of viewing works in the same way that non-Christian works of literature may provide important experiences for the Christian reader. The deconstructionist emphasis on the difficulties of language communication, for example, is important for Christian readers to acknowledge, even though they may continue to disagree with the basic premises on which deconstructionism is built (Longman III 43-44). What is important, however, is that the Christian reader, in the words of T. S. Eliot, needs to bring to reading "the duty of maintaining consciously certain standards and criteria of criticism over and above those applied by the rest of the world; and that by these criteria and standards everything that we read must be tested" (29).

CHAPTER FOUR
SEVENTH-DAY ADVENTISTS, LITERATURE, AND ELLEN WHITE

One might wonder why it is appropriate to center special attention on Seventh-day Adventists and their relationship to the reading and teaching of literature. Why cannot the many books and articles written by committed Christian literature teachers and researchers suffice for advice to Seventh-day Adventist teachers and students? The answer to this question resides in the peculiar history of the Seventh-day Adventist Church and its development over the last nearly one hundred and sixty years.

The Seventh-day Adventist Church grew out of the Millerite Movement in the New England area of the United States during the middle decades (the 30s, 40s, and 50s) of the nineteenth century. As an American religion in its roots, Seventh-day Adventism was heavily influenced by the conservative religious culture within which it developed. In their attitudes towards literature and the arts, early Seventh-day Adventists often revealed perspectives that were not at all original or revolutionary but were, instead, continuations of prevailing religious opinion of the day. Just as the most influential Puritan colonizers of New England had been antagonistic to imaginative literature and to the theater in the 1600s, so their religious descendants of two hundred years later continued to see the arts as dangerous and perhaps antagonistic to spiritual development. Fiction, in particular, was widely perceived as reading which degraded morals and weakened the intellect. James Hart notes that at the beginning of the nineteenth century, various American publications printed an article entitled "Novel Reading a Cause of Female Depravity." Prevailing opinion considered that fiction "'pollutes the imaginations'" and gives youth "'false ideas of life.'" Even the commencement oration at Harvard University in 1803 contained an attack against "the dangers of fiction" (53-54). Similarly, so strong were religious views against the dangers of the theater that no public theatrical entertainments were possible in New

England until the 1780s, even though other sections of the country allowed theatrical productions for most of the eighteenth century (Quinn 115).

Ellen White and Literature

Most of the pioneers of the Seventh-day Adventist Church were originally members of conservative New England Protestant congregations—the Baptists, the Seventh Day Baptists, the Methodists, and the Christian Connection (Maxwell 113)—and imbibed an atmosphere of antagonism towards and distrust of the arts. It is no surprise, therefore, to find that Ellen G. White, from a Methodist background, reveals a very conservative and usually negative attitude towards fiction and drama. What is surprising is that Ellen White continued to hold such views long after the conservative churches of her childhood had modified their views on fiction and theater. In other words, as many nineteenth-century conservative Protestant denominations became more open to the values of reading fiction and viewing drama, Ellen White continued to hold carefully to their original distrustful attitudes.[8] Since the Seventh-day Adventist Church believes that Ellen White was a modern prophet who functioned as a messenger from God, her writings, although not equal to the Bible, have achieved a special status among church members. It is this unique authority of her comments that continues to provide guidance to Seventh-day Adventists in all aspects of life, including reading. Much of the attention of professional Seventh-day Adventist teachers of literature has, therefore, centered on the comments of Ellen White in relation to fiction and drama, genres of literature that have been particularly central to modern audiences.

Ellen White's comments about reading and fiction remained remarkably consistent throughout her life. W. P. Bradley, at the time Chairman of the Board of the White Estate, in a 1971 presentation to the Committee on the Teaching of Literature in Washington, D.C. (reprinted in Dunn, *Seventh-day Adventists on Literature*), noted that "in the *Index* [*to the Writings of Ellen G. White*] one finds about 16 references listed against 'fiction,' and about 28 different references against the novel [...]" (66). The earliest reference, notes Bradley, was published in 1855 and counseled against the "reading of storybooks, foolish stories, and idle tales" (69). Fifty years later, Ellen White

---

[8] John O. Waller explores some of the changing views of nineteenth-century conservative American Christians towards fiction in his article "A Contextual Study of Ellen G. White's Counsel Concerning Fiction."

continued to warn against such reading. "Through the agency of novels and story magazines, Satan is working to fill with unreal and trivial thoughts, minds that should be diligently studying the word of God" (*Counsels to Parents, Teachers, and Students Regarding Christian Education* 121).

Perhaps Ellen White's most negative statements are collected in a chapter entitled "Profitable Study" in *Counsels to Parents, Teachers, and Students Regarding Christian Education* (1913). Here she attacks the "classics" of "Greek and Latin" as taught to "thousands of youth" in higher education, for "while they [the youth] are engaged in these studies, mind and character are molded by the evil sentiments of pagan literature, the reading of which is generally regarded as an essential part of the study of these languages" (381). She then turns attention to fiction and admits that some of these works "written for the purpose of teaching truth or exposing some great evil [...] have accomplished good." But at the same time, "they have also wrought untold harm" since they "contain statements and highly wrought pen pictures that excite the imagination and give rise to a train of thought which is full of danger [...]." This type of "reading unfits the mind for usefulness and disqualifies it for spiritual exercise. It destroys interest in the Bible." She goes on to emphasize that "the reading of fiction" "for mere amusement" inevitably "creates a distaste for life's practical duties." It causes "mental and physical disease," for "the habit of novel reading" can result in invalidism and insanity (383).

She ends this section of her counsels on reading with this forthright statement:

> It is often urged that in order to win the youth from sensational or worthless literature, we should supply them with a better class of fiction. This is like trying to cure a drunkard by giving him, in the place of whisky or brandy, the milder intoxicants, such as wine, beer, or cider. The use of these would continually foster the appetite for stronger stimulants. The only safety for the inebriate, and the only safeguard for the temperate man, is total abstinence. For the lover of fiction the same rule holds true. Total abstinence is his only safety. (383-84)

Just as Ellen White's comments about fiction and novels were unswerving in their expression about the dangers of such reading, so her comments about the theater and drama, though not so numerous, were consistently critical over her career as an Adventist leader. Her earliest statement, published in 1866, attacked the "theatricals" at the health institute in Dansville, while as late as 1905, almost forty years later, she continues to condemn the theater in an article in the *Signs of the Times* (Davis 20).[9] Her most blatant statement of concern, however, appeared as a part of *Testimony 30*, entitled "Proper Education," first published in 1881:

> Among the most dangerous resorts for pleasure is the theater. Instead of being a school of morality and virtue, as is so often claimed, it is the very hotbed of immorality.[…] There is no influence in our land more powerful to poison the imagination, to destroy religious impressions, and to blunt the relish for the tranquil pleasures and sober realities of life than theatrical amusements. The love for these scenes increases with every indulgence, as the desire for intoxicating drink strengthens with its use. The only safe course is to shun the theater […]." (*Testimonies for the Church*, Vol. 4, 652-53)

Ellen White's comments about fiction and the theater (drama) are so pointed and consistently negative that it is little wonder that Seventh-day Adventist Church leaders and literature teachers have directed considerable energy over the decades to evaluating her comments in relationship to their implications for education and for leisure-time activities. It is important to note, however, that while Ellen White specifically condemns fiction-reading and theatrical performances, she also writes certain balancing statements that provide support for what teachers of literature attempt to accomplish in the classroom. In the book *Education*, for example, she notes: "True education does not ignore the value of scientific knowledge or literary acquirements: but above information it values power; above power, goodness; above intellectual acquirement, character" (225). And in *Counsels to Parents, Teachers, and Students Regarding Christian Education*, in a section devoted to preparing students to enter the Loma Linda College of Medical Evangelists, she writes that "inasmuch as there are legal requirements making it necessary that medical students shall take a certain preparatory course of study, our colleges should arrange to carry their students to the point of literary and scientific training that is necessary" (480). When one accepts the likelihood that a student's use of language and writing can be improved by the study of the best literary examples, the following comment from *Education* becomes particularly significant:

---

[9] See my article entitled "Hotbed of Immorality," *Adventist Heritage* 7 (Spring 1982): 20-33, for an analysis of Ellen White's statements in relationship to theatrical productions in Battle Creek.

More important than the acquirement of foreign languages, living or dead, is the ability to write and speak one's mother tongue with ease and accuracy; but no training gained through a knowledge of grammatical rules can compare in importance with the study of language from a higher point of view. With this study, to a great degree, is bound up life's weal or woe. (234)

Finally, it is important to remember that when Ellen White wrote most of her comments about reading fiction and attending the theater, literature teaching (meaning the teaching of English and American literature for its own sake) was really only in its infancy in the United States. Fiction and novels were still suspect, though less on religious grounds than on artistic grounds, and were usually excluded from the literature curriculum for reasons of lack of artistic merit. Poetry was the most likely center of attention in the literature classroom, and Ellen White never condemns poetry-reading as such. The nineteenth-century popular theater in America, moreover, was mired in escapist and sensational melodrama. All this is to say that Ellen White's comments were directed less at the literature classroom than at leisure-time activities of church members who, evidently, were devoting more than a little time to reading fiction and attending live theater performances which Ellen White found objectionable. But, of course, the development of literary studies during the twentieth century has resulted in an elevation of fiction and drama to central places in the literature curriculum, thus making the statements of Ellen White crucial as Seventh-day Adventist literature teachers attempt to wrestle with what constitutes good reading or appropriate entertainment for their students.

The Precedent of Early Seventh-day Adventist Literature Teachers: Bell and Rine

Early Seventh-day Adventist literature teachers carefully cultivated a conservative and moralistic approach to their teaching of literature in denominational schools. The most influential of these teachers, Professor Goodloe Harper Bell (1832-1899), taught the children of Ellen and James White in Battle Creek in the little school which they helped to set up and then became one of the most forceful members of the faculty when that school developed into the first Seventh-day Adventist institution of higher learning, Battle Creek College, in 1874.

Because of Bell's extensive writing, it is possible to have a clear idea of his views on teaching literature. These views are expressed most effectively and completely in his textbook entitled *Studies in English and American*

Literature, published in 1900, just after Bell's death, by a non-denominational publishing company in Chicago. Bell specifically develops ideas that coincide with the moral criticism of his day (see Chapter Two). The purpose for studying literature is to "become acquainted with the best thoughts of its [a nation's] best minds." Such reading provides "the highest ideals and the noblest motives" and "fosters a love for pure thoughts and beautiful expression," thus resulting in "a distaste for whatever is low or unworthy." "Thus one comes at length to turn from coarse or worthless reading as instinctively as from vulgar society" (19). Bell is concerned that students learn to develop their own "taste" so that they "will be able to discriminate at once between real literature and trash." He notes that the time will come when students will not "have parents, teachers, or friends by their side to tell them whether or not a book is good reading. They must learn to recognize for themselves the *moral tendency* [italics added for emphasis], the literary character, the trend of influence, which constitute the inherent power for good or evil of any piece of writing" (6).

It is particularly enlightening to review Bell's *Studies in English and American Literature* in relationship to Ellen White's comments about fiction and the theater. Bell never mentions either genre by name in his textbook, nor does he include any selection from drama or the theater, including Shakespeare. Instead, the anthology section of his text is divided thematically into sections such as "In Honor of the Creator," "Education, Morals, and Religion," "Studies in Nature," "Home Scenes and Influences," and "Studies in Character" (12-15). There are numerous poetry selections, some by such well-known writers as Robert Burns, William Wordsworth, Alfred Lord Tennyson, William Cullen Bryant, and Henry Wadsworth Longfellow.

The prose selections are generally limited to a few paragraphs from longer works. Many of these are from religious writers, little known today, including two offerings from Ellen White, both centering on King David's life, selected from her writings collected as *The Story of Patriarchs and Prophets*, although Bell does not provide any information about the author herself in his outline of the development of literature in English.

Even though Bell does not address fiction specifically in his comments about literature, he does include some selections which clearly come from fictional works. He does not always identify the titles of the larger works of fiction from which he selects his sample paragraphs, however, although he does clearly label the authors of the literary samples. Included are selections which come from the fictional narrative literature of such authors as Oliver Goldsmith, George Eliot, Nathaniel Hawthorne, James Fenimore Cooper, Harriet Beecher Stowe, and Charles Dickens.[10]

Bell's willingness to include items from clearly fictional works indicates that he was unwilling to eliminate that genre of literature from school study, even though he was well-acquainted with Ellen White and her statements about fiction. As such, he set the pattern for later teachers of literature who continuously have interpreted her writings about fiction and theater as not really intending a complete elimination of such works from one's reading. Even so, however, Bell's selections in his *Studies in English and American Literature* are heavily tilted towards poetry and non-fiction prose.

An emphasis on poetry was central also to another early Seventh-day Adventist literature teacher, George Washington Rine (1850-1938), who taught in California at Healdsburg College and its successor Pacific Union College during the years when Ellen White resided close by.

Rine's nineteen articles on literature were published in the denomination's official publication for young people, *The Youth's Instructor*, during 1898 and 1899, while Rine was teaching at Healdsburg College in California.[11] An Ellen White devotional article appears in every issue that includes a Rine contribution. What is fascinating is that Rine uses a fictional framework for his articles, evidently as an attempt to pique reader interest. He invents a professor ("Professor James R. Woodrow"), a group of student characters, and a high school ("Ebbensville High School") to provide the possibility for classroom dialogue about literary topics. Unlike Bell, Rine was convinced of the importance of learning about the lives of authors as well as becoming acquainted with their works. His college education in Pennsylvania had made necessary such an approach (Waller, "Some Roots" 129-130), and he lists thirteen American writers whom high school students should read. The articles are developed through concentration on these particular American writers (the fictional class group decides that they would prefer to study about authors from their

---

[10]See *Studies in English and American Literature*, pages 343-346, 356-357, 369-372, 401-403, 404-407, and 407-412.

[11]At the time, *The Youth's Instructor* published regular features on a variety of topics such as music, travel, history, nature, and physical culture. Rine's series of nineteen articles on literature began to appear on May 26, 1898, and continued at regular intervals through the March 2, 1899, issue. A few of the articles were lengthy enough to be continued in more than one issue, however. In the course of the articles, Rine covers thirteen American writers. Three of the articles are not centered on individual writers—one on poetry and two on words.

own country before learning about British writers) with Professor Woodrow posing apt questions and students responding, often in the form of supposed student research presented in an oral report ("Washington Irving" 401). Like Bell, Rine values poetry highly. One article, "Poetry: Its Nature and Mission," clearly emphasizes Rine's moralistic critical leanings, for the best poetry provides a "refined, spiritual pleasure which beautifies and expands the soul and warms and deepens the sympathies" and "the mission of poetry is to enable those who have eyes and see not, and ears, but hear not, to perceive and enjoy the beauty and the eternal meaning which God has put into all his works [...]" (434-435). Of the thirteen writers included in the articles, eight are primarily known as poets, including William C. Bryant, Henry W. Longfellow, John G. Whittier, Oliver W. Holmes, and James R. Lowell. Three of the writers are praised primarily for their non-fiction prose: Henry D. Thoreau, the historian George C. Bancroft, and the journalist/essayist Charles D. Warner.

What is most interesting, however, is that two of the writers covered by Rine are primarily known as writers of fiction: Washington Irving and Nathaniel Hawthorne.[12] Rine never mentions the word "fiction" with either writer. He emphasizes that Irving is "the father of our country's literature" ("Washington Irving" 401) and praises Irving's *The Sketch Book*, including "The Legend of Sleepy Hollow" and "Rip Van Winkle" (403). Rine also praises Hawthorne's prose as including "everything of poetry but meter" ("Nathaniel Hawthorne" 603), centering particular attention on the children's books (*Tanglewood Tales* and *The Wonderbook for Boys and Girls*) and on the "historical sketches" in *Mosses from the Old Manse* (602-603). He makes his students less enthusiastic about *The Scarlet Letter*, however, admitting that it is "ranked by many as the author's masterpiece" but that "it deals with facts, however, too obscure, abstract, and weird to suit the taste and culture of average readers" (603). The students do comment on the "artistic excellence" of Hawthorne's "philosophical romances," however, including *The House of the Seven Gables* and *The Marble Faun* (603).[13]

Bell and Rine, both active teachers of literature while Ellen White was still alive, emphasized the moral and uplifting nature of literary study and did not directly address her comments about fiction and the theater. The inclusion by

[12]Two of the other writers, Oliver W. Holmes and Charles D. Warner, also wrote some fiction.

[13]In refusing to use the terms "fiction" or "novel" when treating Hawthorne, Rine was actually following in Hawthorne's footsteps since Hawthorne himself referred to his stories as tales or sketches and to his longer works of fiction as romances.

Bell of some fictional selections in his *English and American Literature* and Rine's willingness to center on some writers of fiction in his articles in *The Youth's Instructor*, however, seem to indicate an implicit assumption that Ellen White's statements about fiction reading did not include a complete banishing of the genre from the reading choices in the curriculum.

Views of Later Seventh-day Adventist Teachers on Reading and Teaching Literature

After Ellen White's death in 1915, her writings began to assume a more central position in American Seventh-day Adventist circles than they did in her lifetime. Such centrality was furthered by the growth in influence of the Ellen G. White Estate as it continued the publication and supervision of her publications and by the structured study of her prophetic authority in Sabbath School lessons and in the curriculum of denominational schools. As a result, her comments on fiction reading and on theater attendance became even more well-known and crucial than they had been when first issued while she was still alive. Inevitably, the result in the United States was that Seventh-day Adventist teachers of literature were faced with serious questions about reading choices at the very time modern fiction and drama were becoming more and more central to the literature curriculum of twentieth-century schools.

It was not until after World War II, however, that such teachers began to voice and publish materials which specifically addressed her comments in any concerted way. Between World War II and the issuance of the official "Guide to the Teaching of Literature in Seventh-day Adventist Schools" in 1971 by the Department of Education of the General Conference of Seventh-day Adventists, several Seventh-day Adventist teachers of literature seriously considered Ellen White's statements about reading, although there was some disagreement about how best to interpret her comments.

Professor L. W. Cobb and a "Literal Reading" of Ellen White

The teacher and writer who took the most conservative view of reading in relationship to Ellen White's statements was L. W. Cobb (1882-1985).[14]

---

[14]Professor Cobb, who received his M.A. from the University of Nebraska in 1915, served as a teacher of English and as an administrator at several Seventh-day Adventist colleges over his career, including Canadian Junior College, Pacific Union College, Union College, and Washington Missionary College. Cobb's most complete statement of his ideas about reading was not issued until he was in his eighties in 1966 and he self-published

Give Attendance to Reading (1966), the title of Cobb's primary work on literature study, comes from Paul's writing in 1 Timothy 4:13: "Till I come, give attendance to reading, to exhortation, to doctrine." Cobb emphasizes that Paul's advice to Timothy underscores the rich "possibilities" of not only "reading the Bible" but also "secular reading as well." But, reminds Cobb, "'Give attendance to reading'" also implies the need for "protective limitations" since reading has inherent dangers. Ellen White's "counsels on books and reading [...] are given to draw a line between good and bad, between suitable reading matter and unsuitable, and to give guidance and warning that are needed" (7).

The rest of the book is Cobb's unremitting attempt to interpret Ellen White's statements as literally as possible and rigidly to apply these statements to literature teaching and to reading choices. His approach begins with the basic premise that, given Ellen White's comments antagonistic to fiction, nothing in the Bible should be classified as fictional. Instead, those parts of the Bible which partake of the traditions of imaginative literature, such as the figurative language ("tropes"), symbolism, or "parables," should be seen as passages developed by the use of "rhetorical figures" and must not be confused with fiction (55). Parable and allegory are distinct from fiction, suggests Cobb, in that their very nature allows for them to be a "most effective means for 'spiritualizing thought [...]'" (58). Even though Christ's parable about "the rich man and Lazarus" (Luke 16:19-31) is not factual from a Seventh-day Adventist point of view in that the story details a picture of life after death contrary to the Seventh-day Adventist view of the state of the dead, Cobb insists that this parable is "'figurative'" rather than fictional; it is "unliteral" rather than "fiction" (59). Cobb can defend Ellen White's appreciation of John Bunyan's *Pilgrim's Progress* on similar grounds, for in his eyes, Bunyan's work is allegorical and not fictional (84). According to Cobb, then, the term "fiction" must be understood rather narrowly as having to do with "a false statement" or with things that are "feigned." In relationship to literature, the term centers on "novels" or modern short stories (60, 64). Cobb sketches the history of the novel with particular

---

his little book *Give Attendance to Reading*, although one can safely assume that his views in that book are consistent with his ideas and practices throughout his lengthy educational career because of the "pasted-in" preface, entitled "ABOUT THIS BOOK." In that preface, Cobb indicates that the book's "contents were drawn from my experience of forty years in Seventh-day Adventist educational work."

emphasis on his view that there are no good novels for the Christian, even though some have tried to distinguish between "the sensational dime novel" and more serious artistic attempts. He particularly is at pains to point out how Ellen White's statements, issued over more than "fifty years," coincided with the serious artistic efforts of the best novel writers (he lists the authors and their works), what he calls the "golden age of the novel" (61-62). His point here is that Ellen White "was commissioned" to warn readers of the dangers of all novel-reading, including the products of the most artistic and serious writers of fiction of her time (62-63).

Since Ellen White does not condemn poetry as a genre in the way she seemingly condemns fiction, Cobb is forced to recognize that narratives in poetry can also be fictional, the only difference being verse as opposed to prose. Given Ellen White's silence on poetry, Cobb is willing to make some allowance for reading certain stories or narratives in verse, although he never clarifies just why *some* verse fiction should be allowable while *all* prose fiction is not (66). Apparently, also, non-narrative poetry (lyric poetry, for example), since it is not fictional in Cobb's sense of the word, can be included in literature study for the classroom. Cobb's understanding of Ellen White's view leaves very little in the way of imaginative literature from which the modern Seventh-day Adventist teacher of literature can choose. As a long-time educator, however, he seemingly recognized the need to inform students, particularly English majors, about the very literature that Ellen White disallowed. Thus, his strategy for teaching literature emphasized *not the reading of fiction* but instead *the reading and learning about fiction.* His classroom practices, therefore, depended on his providing outlines and lectures about fiction and novels and in assigning students the reading of plot summaries and secondary sources which discussed the meaning and artistic tools employed by fiction writers (42-45). His defense of this methodology is explained in the following analogies: "We do not read books on magic or on the technique of the spiritist medium or on card playing, for example. Instead, we inform ourselves, so that we can warn men effectively against these evils. We may use the same principle in dealing with other objectionable books" (44-45).

There are a number of objections that can be safely raised to Cobb's approach to literature as detailed in *Give Attendance to Reading*. First and foremost, the approach is characterized by a certain negative tone, perhaps inevitable given his concern to stress how fiction and novels by their very form (even though never defined sufficiently) damage Christian experience. It is difficult to find in his book any really positive statements about literature and its effects on the reader, even though he does admit in one place the transforming power of such reading: "Literature is mainly a record of the world within. Great literature, 'the literature of power,' is dynamic. Rightly administered, it means not only increase in knowledge but transformation. Our supreme concern is to bring about growth in the student—mental, naturally; more important, spiritual" (49). He goes ahead to note that the few literature selections actually read by students should "be thought of as pearls on a string" with the "'strings'" themselves being made up of "comprehensive outlines, biographical and historical, specifically prepared by us" so that "the student may see the relation of a writer to what were then issues in the conflict" "between good and evil" (49). And the feeling one gets from Cobb's book is that in handling literature in the classroom, most of the teacher's time will be spent in pointing out the evil of literature, often read only in short, second-hand summary form, rather than the good.

A second concern is that Cobb never really comes to grips with the changing and complex nature of the terms "fiction," "novel," and "story." He seems to believe that these categories are easy to label and carry self-evident definitions. He evidently believes that Ellen White had a consistent definition in mind as she wrote. His attempt to separate parable and allegory from literature that is fictional is a beginning towards wrestling with the term "fiction" itself, but he stops his definitions at that point, seemingly assured that on such grounds Ellen White's comments can best be understood as disallowing all fiction from the Christian reader's choice of selections. Similarly, his unwillingness to condemn all fictional stories in poetry in the same way that he condemns all prose fiction seems at best inconsistent.

Finally, his classroom methodology which emphasizes that it is acceptable and necessary to inform students about authors and works of fiction and that allows them to read plot summaries and outlines of such works seems mildly contradictory. Why is reading a short version better than reading the full work? Evidently, it has something to do with time spent and with the possibility that the original work has snares and temptations that a plot summary does not contain. Such an approach does not seem terribly convincing since the content of such fictional works, with all the possible evils described in digested form, would still seem to present some problems for spiritual growth, even though the charms of the original language may be obscured by the plodding language of plot summary. Cobb seems to believe that this second-hand approach to learning about literature is perfectly acceptable, although admittedly somewhat of a "handicap," yet a necessary Christian sacrifice which should result in educating students to a sufficient professional level of knowledge about literature (45). It is ironic that Cobb's approach to teaching literature, an approach that distances students from primary texts as much as possible, was published in its final revised form right at the end of nearly forty years of growing emphasis in the United States and Britain on the necessity of students having immediate contact with literary texts. The New Criticism (see Chapter Two) consistently emphasized that students must learn to analyze texts for themselves, without the crutch of secondary sources. In 1915, when Cobb received his graduate degree, it might have been possible to maintain a somewhat remote distance from literary texts, even at the graduate level. In 1966, when the hardback version of his book was finally published, such an approach was impossible. Cobb, who had been retired for around twenty years at the time, seems not to have been aware of the changes in literary criticism and classroom approaches that occurred during the decades in which he was perfecting his classroom practices.

Ellen White in Context: Professor Harry M. Tippett

In a sense, L. W. Cobb's stance is a lonely voice among the statements of post-World War II Seventh-day Adventist English teachers. The other writers who addressed the comments of Ellen White did so in a more analytical way—that is, they attempted to place her comments into the historical and textual context of her statements with special consideration of the complex nuances and dynamic, changing nature of the terms "fiction," "novels," and "theater."

In 1949, Harry M. Tippett, former chair of the English Department at Emmanuel Missionary College (1926-1946) and at the time an associate book editor at the Review and Herald Publishing Company, delivered a paper at the Seventh-day Adventist Council of College English Teachers, entitled "A Review of Some Principles in Dealing with Fiction and Imaginative Forms of Literature in Our Schools," a wide-ranging and common sense approach to the dilemmas of teaching literature in a Seventh-day Adventist context, given the comments of Ellen White.[15] The first question that Tippett addresses is "'What is truth?'" His

---

[15] Tippett had received the M.A. in English at the University of Michigan, followed by further graduate study at the University of Notre Dame and at Northwestern University. He authored several devotional books while functioning as a book editor at the Review and Herald Publishing Company. After World War II, the North American Division of the General Conference set up a system of regular meetings of Seventh-day Adventist college teachers in various localities throughout the United States, usually at intervals of four or five years.

concern is to emphasize that truth for the Christian is more than mere fact. His touchstone is Christ. "If truth was embodied in Christ, then it must be godlike, for He was like God. Truth must square with the moral law, with spiritual law, with physical law, and with the laws of the mind, for the life and chracter [sic] of Jesus did" (91). Even a factual biography may not be "true" in this sense. Just as important, says Tippett, "How shall we say that truth is bound to factual accounts and cannot be illuminated with idealizations of life in story form?" Indeed, "truth is so great in concept, we can not apprehend it in toto"; nor can it be confined to any literary form (92). Hence, fiction as form should not be excluded from reading choices. "What I am trying to set forth," continues Tippett, "is that a piece of literature is not good or bad because it falls into a certain category in classification of its form" (92). Tippett stands against those (like Cobb) who claim that *Pilgrim's Progress* and the biblical parable of the Rich Man and Lazarus are not fiction (92-93). On the other hand, recognizing that fiction as a form should not be dismissed does not mean that just any fiction is worth reading, for "I fear many a modern novel and piece of drama is read and perhaps assigned to classes for study with the ostensible purpose of getting at the moral values in it, but in doing so one is dragged through so much of the nasty and putrid that the terminal values are well-nigh obscured" (92). But Tippett "can not go along with those who say or believe that imaginative forms of literature are evil per se and in toto" (93). Indeed, he claims that "an old worker in our [the Seventh-day Adventist] cause" pictured Ellen White "sitting on the floor of her parlor with magazines and books scattered about her from which she clipped articles and stories that were chosen for our youth to read," the collection of materials that eventually made up *Sabbath Readings for the Home Circle*, issued in 1905. The stories in this collection "were true to life, to probity, to honor, to virtue" but were not "all factual accounts of actual happenings" (94).[16]

Tippett ends his presentation with an emphasis on how literature must be chosen carefully in relationship to the highest standards of truth and not in relationship to its form alone. "The Christian [...] should best be able to judge what true art means, for he is nearest in understanding of the great master Artist Himself." He has not intended his paper to be "a plea for the novel" or as a "skirting of the plain counsel of the Spirit of Prophecy [the

---

[16]Tippett's statements about the contents of Ellen White's collection of readings for youth are the first in a series of reactions from literature teachers over the next two decades.

comments of Ellen White]," but rather, he claims, what he has attempted is to emphasize the "great responsibility […] laid upon the individual teacher to seek that wisdom from above in keeping the margins wide between what we approve and what we disapprove" (96).

Ellen White Comments Analyzed: Dr. Paul T. Gibbs

Eleven years after Tippett's presentation in 1949, in August 1961, Dr. Paul T. Gibbs, chair of the English Department at the newly formed Andrews University, presented a paper entitled "Literature in Adventist Schools" to another gathering of English teachers at Southern Missionary College.[17] Whereas Tippett in his presentation had not directly and specifically reacted to Ellen White comments on literature, but had instead emphasized in rather general terms the importance of distinguishing between truth and fact, Gibbs was evidently commissioned prior to the 1961 meetings to take on the "assignment […] to reexamine Mrs. E. G. White's teaching on the selection of literature for Adventist schools […]" (113). What follows is a fairly specific attempt by Gibbs to examine some Ellen White comments on literature in a balanced and logical manner, trying to explain their meaning and interpretation.

In the first part of his argument, Gibbs is at pains to begin with Ellen White quotations that emphasize the importance of "'<u>literary acquirements,</u>'" but he follows this section with that most damaging comment by Ellen White against fiction from *Counsels to Parents, Teachers, and Students Regarding Christian Education* (383-384), which ends with this abrupt statement: "'Total abstinence [from fiction reading] is his [the fiction reader's] only safety'" (114-115). He attempts to put this statement into appropriate perspective by (first) emphasizing that just as with the Bible one text must be read in the context of other texts, so with Ellen White, one comment must be read in relationship to other comments. He next specifies that dictionary definitions of fiction are not very helpful in trying to understand what Ellen White meant by the term. Instead, Gibbs constructs his own version of Ellen White's definition of fiction from the many comments and their contexts in her writings. "I believe Mrs. White meant by <u>fiction</u> what the word most frequently stands for in the mind of the man or woman in the market place or in the kitchen—plotted stories of carnal love, greed, temper—the lurid, cheap magazine story" (115-116).

---

[17]Gibbs took his doctoral work at the University of Michigan. He chaired the English Department at Emmanuel Missionary College (later Andrews University) until 1963.

He agrees with Ellen White that some "people are addicted to this sort of reading" and that such people would benefit from total abstinence. These are the people, he suggests, for whom the damaging comment about fiction (cited above) was written. But "less than one in a thousand of my students" are this type of person, says Gibbs (116).

As a result, Gibbs does not believe that Ellen White intended to exclude such works as "The Great Stone Face, Rip Van Winkle, the Headless Horseman, Evangeline, Beowulf or Twelfth Night" from the reading choices available to teachers and students.[18] Gibbs observes that when he assigns such reading, rather than encouraging a drunkard-like addiction to fiction, he has often "had to whip the sluggard to his task" and has "been tempted to wish my class materials were more fascinating" (116). Gibbs points out that Ellen White never offered a list of authors or works that should not be read, perhaps for the reason that "circumstances differ" for various people, making such a list inappropriate. Just as a missionary to "a Moslem country" might benefit from reading "the Koran," while another reader would not benefit from such reading, so with various literary works and various kinds of students. Appropriately, "an Adventist youth is correct in reading many things under the guidance of a mature Christian teacher that he should not undertake by himself" (116).

Like Tippett, Dr. Gibbs also classifies *Pilgrim's Progress* and the parable of the Rich Man and Lazarus as fictional, and he cites Ellen White's compilation of stories for *Sabbath Readings for the Home Circle* as evidence that her comments on fiction should not indicate a total prohibition on reading all fictional works (117-118). He indicates that he has examined the stories in her compilation for youth and has concluded that there are works included that "are fiction," but that such inclusion was in no way a contradiction of Ellen White's stance on reading, for her definition of fiction apparently did not include the type of stories she chose for her anthology (118-119).

Gibbs expresses reservations about constructing "one list" of appropriate selections "for all teachers" (129).[19] Instead, near the end of his presentation, Gibbs provides these general statements about reading choices:

---

[18]Gibbs uses this unusual underlining of short story and poem titles in his paper. He probably means Irving's "The Legend of Sleepy Hollow" when he refers to "The Headless Horseman."

[19]Interestingly, a year later, in 1962, Gibbs participated in issuing such a list for secondary teachers, entitled "Recommended Imaginative Reading for Secondary Schools." The majority of the nearly 270 prose works on this list are fictional.

The kind and amount of thinking caused by any piece of reading is a good test of its merits. Some reading stimulates little thought of any kind; it is bad for that reason. A selection that induces constructive, wholesome thinking is probably worthy. Literature should present fact or truth or both. Truth versus error is a more reliable basis of choice than fact versus fiction. Much factual material is most unwholesome, while fiction can present truth. Literature should be selected that tends to make work-a-day work more attractive, not less. It should make the Bible and Sabbath School more satisfying rather than less. But there will always be differences, I believe, between teacher and teacher, in what authors and what selections do this. (129)

Ellen White in the Context of Nineteenth-Century Attitudes Towards Fiction: Dr. John O. Waller

Dr. Paul Gibbs's study addresses the comments of Ellen White through a careful review of what the comments say and what specific contexts surround the statements. Like Professor Tippett, Gibbs cites in particular Ellen White's compilation of *Sabbath Readings for the Home Circle* as evidence that she had not intended a complete prohibition of the reading of fiction. Dr. John O. Waller, Gibbs's successor as chair of the English Department at Andrews University, went much further than either Professor Tippett or Dr. Gibbs in his attempt to research in a careful and methodical manner the cultural contexts surrounding Ellen White's comments on fiction and her method of making selections for her anthology of stories for young people.[20] Waller presented his paper, "A Contextual Study of Ellen G. White's Counsel Concerning Fiction," to the quadrennial section meeting of Seventh-day Adventist English teachers, meeting at La Sierra College, in August 1965.[21] This paper has become the most influential of all the studies on Ellen White and literature and has paved the way for the practices of Seventh-day Adventist literature teachers in the United States during the past three decades.[22]

---

[20]Dr. Waller's graduate degrees came from the University of Southern California.

[21]Like Gibbs, Waller was very concerned about how his study of Ellen White's counsel on fiction might be understood or misunderstood. He refused actual publication of the paper for nearly ten years, before it appeared in Robert Dunn's collection of materials about reading literature, entitled *Seventh-day Adventists on Literature*, published in 1974.

[22]Waller's paper did not end Seventh-day Adventist literature teachers' desire to write about Ellen White's comments on literature. In 1982, for example, my article on Ellen White's counsels about the theater, entitled "Hotbed of Immorality," attempted to analyze the context of her statements about drama. Similarly, several of the essays by the

Waller begins his paper by underscoring his allegiance to Ellen White and her leadership in the Seventh-day Adventist Church, including his desire to follow her "counsel" regarding fiction. "The only legitimate questions," he insists, "concern what the counsel means" (47). He underscores that he believes that Mrs. White "was consistent in following her deepest convictions and the special light she received" and that he hopes that nobody will "draw overly liberal implications" from his presentation (49). Waller then sets out to contextualize the statements of Ellen White. He does so first by tracing his research on the changing nineteenth-century conservative protestant views of fiction in the United States. He notes in particular that the Methodist Church, the religion of Ellen White in her youth, moved from condemnation of the novel and fiction in the early 1800s to provisional recommendations of certain novels at mid-century to finally underscoring in 1900 the "duty of every minister to be acquainted with the best American and English novels" (50-51). But though conservative denominations changed their views on reading during the nineteenth century, "Mrs. White stood steadfast against the tide [...]" (51). Waller is at pains to emphasize that what particularly concerned Ellen White and other writers about fiction in the nineteenth century was "the problem of compulsive novel-reading, the insatiable hunger for poring over novel after novel to the neglect of prayer, Bible study, or practical activity of any sort" (52). After reviewing some of the typical statements written by contemporaries of Ellen White concerning this addiction to fiction, Waller notes that probably the problem of such "compulsive fiction-reading" has decreased in the twentieth century as the market for magazine fiction has decreased. However, he emphasizes that the replacement for such addictive reading is now addiction to the popular media—radio, television, and the movies: "But don't you suppose that the

---

literature-teaching participants in the International Faith and Learning Seminars (sponsored by the Education Department of the General Conference of Seventh-day Adventists) over the past fourteen years have emphasized Ellen White comments and how they should be understood in relationship to literary studies. See, for example, David Velez-Sepulveda's "Literature and Life: Teaching Fictional Literature in Adventist Higher Education," and Shirley McGarrell's "Faith and Fiction: An Inspiring Dilemma for Seventh-day Adventist Teachers of Literature." Scott Moncrieff's "Adventists and fiction: Another look" also directs attention to Ellen White statements, although the main thrust of the article points out how writers of narration based on fact and writers of fiction must rely on similar approaches and skills. Thus, Moncrieff can confidently proclaim that "[Seventh-day Adventist] church members do write novels and Adventist presses do publish them" (9).

grandchildren and great-grandchildren of the 1900-style fiction fiend are sitting somewhere in semi-darkness, eyes hypnotically transfixed upon the flickering television screen?" (53-54).

Waller then turns attention to analyzing what Mrs. White may have meant by the term "fiction" itself. He emphasizes that very often the Ellen White statements about fiction carry within them clear identifications of what she meant with descriptive terms such as "cheap" or "trashy" as modifiers. He believes that it is "sheer perversity" to enlarge such statements into general condemnations of all fiction. But, he admits, there are other statements that speak more "broadly of 'fiction'" (54). What about these counsels?

Waller underscores that "the English language itself is notoriously ambiguous" in its terminology regarding fiction. "Our language is deficient in single precise generic terms applicable to fictional literature; the terms notoriously overlap" (54). He cites the attempt in the last century to distinguish between the romance and the novel, a distinction that "never really caught on with ordinary people […]" (55). Fiction as a term, therefore, casts a very wide net and has been applied to "both novels and romances" as well as to "short stories and narrative poems," making it difficult for writers and readers to understand clearly what is meant when the term is used.

Such imprecision makes it doubly difficult to understand what Ellen White means when she uses the term, although Waller believes that Ellen White's prohibition against the reading of fiction did not include "'simple tales, where the narrative is employed for no other purpose but that of giving occasion for sentiments which the author is anxious to introduce and enforce'" (55-56). Waller bases such a conclusion about Ellen White's view of fiction on his painstaking research regarding Ellen White's compilation of stories for her *Sabbath Readings for the Home Circle*. Perhaps following the suggestive statements of Professor Tippett and Dr. Gibbs regarding the inclusion of some fictional stories in this collection (see above), Waller determined to search out the original publications in which the stories appeared to determine whether or not they were fiction. He "examined one hundred ninety-four stories" attempting to identify their authorship or the original source of publication (56). He notes that a few were from "well-known fiction writers of their day, including Hans Christian Anderson and Harriet Beecher Stowe […]" (56). He was not very successful in identifying the authors of the other stories, since most of them were originally published anonymously, although he was able to verify the original publications in which they appeared. In total, he concludes that ninety-nine stories came from upwards of seventy-one different magazines, "several of which were known primarily as fiction magazines" (57). In order for Ellen White "to verify the true-to-fact bases for all these stories," she would have had to send letters to all the publishers and editors "of perhaps a hundred different publications assuring her that they never published any nonfactual stories in their papers" (57). There is no evidence that such was done. One must conclude, then, that "she approved of many stories concerning which she could have had no certainty that they were true-to-fact" (57). Hence, her "counsels against the reading of fiction" do not include the type of narratives which she included in her own anthology for youth (57).

What Waller concludes from his study of Ellen White and fiction is that her very act of culling through hundreds of stories in order to choose the relatively few for her *Sabbath Readings for the Home Circle* can become a model for what the Christian teacher of literature must do in the selection of reading for class use, for "she established the principle of exercising moral discrimination in dealing with simple, clearly moralistic fiction" (59). What is most important, Waller emphasizes, is that Ellen White would only approve of "a critical approach" to reading, "an approach in which the reading is not for the story alone, in which the mind is in no sense merely passive, an informed and methodical kind of study" (59). With such an approach, the college English teacher may safely "introduce some fiction" (59).

The 1971 General Conference-Approved "Guide to the Teaching of Literature in Seventh-day Adventist Schools"

Dr. John Waller's paper on Ellen White and fiction, although not published until nine years after its first presentation, received fairly wide distribution by means of follow-up lectures on various college campuses and through duplication of the original. His conclusion that Ellen White had approved of some fiction in her own collections of materials for youth provided a sometimes heated discussion point for educational leaders and helped to redefine the Seventh-day Adventist view of literature in the United States. Fiction-selection became the center of a controversy, for example, at the 1968 meetings of North American Seventh-day Adventist higher educational personnel at Andrews University.

There was one important result of the interchanges at these sessions. An official committee was set up to study the selection of literature for classroom use in Seventh-day Adventist schools. Members of the committee included representative teachers and librarians as well as church educational leaders and a representative from the Ellen G. White Estate. The committee met intensively for one week, listened to various presentations regarding reading choice, and issued an official series of guidelines under the auspices of the General Conference Education Department in 1971, after its official adoption at Autumn Council.[23]

The statement, much of which was drafted by Waller, continues to be the most complete, albeit brief, overview of the place of literature in Seventh-day Adventist education. The section on "Philosophy" firmly establishes the statement in the context of moralistic critical approaches to literature by emphasizing that "the teaching of literature in Seventh-day Adventist schools should give primary emphasis to character-building" (114). The counsels of Ellen White support "guided study of secular literature, both the fact-based and some true-to-principle non-fact-based [...]" (114). Besides an emphasis on moral content, however, literature study should also include attention to "aesthetic qualities" and should provide students with models for "their own literary endeavors" (114).

The "Criteria" for literature selection specifies that reading should be "serious art," should "avoid sensationalism," should "not be characterized by profanity or other crude or offensive language," should avoid "making evil desirable or goodness appear trivial," should "avoid simplified, excitingly suspenseful, or plot-dominated stories," and should "be adapted to the maturity level of the group or individual" (115). Particular attention is paid to the term "Fiction," with an emphasis on what Ellen White seemed to mean by the term and a recognition that she herself included some fiction in her own choices of reading for youth (116). Teachers should refrain from "glorifying the authors of literary works" but also recognize that some "ungodly authors" might have written works which can be used in the classroom (116-117). Regardless, however, with all assignments, the "teacher will use materials and methods to assist students in attaining the highest goals God has designed for man" (118) and will always provide "optional acceptable reading on related topics" for students who have "conscientious convictions" against any particular assignment (118). The statement ends with a section on the importance of using literature from

---

[23]The "Guide to the Teaching of Literature in Seventh-day Adventist Schools" is included as Appendix I in the present volume. Page references to the "Guide" are from this Appendix. Its publication date in 1971 meant that its wording does not coincide with present expectations regarding inclusive language.

"Multi-ethnic Groups," emphasizing the importance of recognizing "the pluralistic character of our society" (118-119).[24]

The 1971 "Guide" has for more than thirty years provided a sane and conservative basis for reading choices among Seventh-day Adventist teachers of literature.[25] It contains reasonable guidelines that address issues of genre, modernity, ethnicity, frankness of language, and realism of portrayal. But, of course, as helpful as the "Guide" is, it cannot replace the importance of teacher decision-making in choosing what students will read. Each teacher will interpret the "Guide" in somewhat different ways. A text that one teacher finds perfectly acceptable in relationship to the principles explained in the "Guide" may not seem so to another teacher, to some students, or to parents. The "Guide" itself underscores the importance of the teacher in thinking carefully about making reading selections. The effective instructor "will take into consideration the Adventist constituency in which he teaches, the homes from which the students come, most importantly the students themselves, adapting to their needs." Further, in solving "professional problems" related to reading choices, "the teacher should counsel with his colleagues, and in case of doubt on certain reading material to be presented to or read by the students, he should seek further counsel from the school administration" (118).

---

[24]In spite of the fact that the General Conference Education Department has continuously kept the "Guide" in print and has distributed it without cost for nearly thirty years, the "Guide" is surprisingly little known by many literature teachers. Dr. Shirley McGarrell, for example, in her research for her doctoral dissertation, "Differential Perceptions of English Teachers of Literature in Seventh-day Adventist Secondary Schools in Selected Regions of the Carribean," discovered that none of the Seventh-day Adventist secondary teachers she surveyed in the Carribean area around Trinidad possessed the "Guide" or had any specific knowledge of its contents.

[25]It is also true, however, that the "Guide" probably needs updating, certainly in its outdated non-inclusive language, but also in its handling of the challenges of contemporary theory as well as the realities concerning trends in literature during the past more than thirty years of postmodernism in the arts and the ever-growing importance of Young Adult Literature.

CHAPTER FIVE

SEVENTH-DAY ADVENTISTS AND THE BIBLE AS LITERATURE

The English Bible as Literature: The First Phase

Given the conservative stance of Seventh-day Adventists regarding reading choices, it is not surprising that Seventh-day Adventist literature teachers early embraced a literary approach to the Bible as a helpful and "safe" component of the curriculum. Professor Goodloe Harper Bell sets the tone at the turn of the twentieth century in the "Preface" to his *Studies in English and American Literature*, as he explains how he has chosen the selections for his anthology. "In making selections […] regard has been had to their influence upon mind and character, as well as to their literary merits. Selections have not been made from the Bible—the best of all literature—for the reason that it is in everybody's possession, and can be drawn from at will" (3). What Bell termed "the best of all literature" was echoed by Ellen White in *Education*, published in 1903, when she notes that "the earliest as well as the most sublime of poetic utterances known to man are found in the Scriptures" and underscores the Bible's "fullness," "strength," and "depth of meaning" in contrast to books of lesser "literary value" which students are often encouraged to read (159, 188).

What needs to be emphasized is that Professor Bell and Ellen White were not lonely voices in the United States in their high opinion regarding the English Bible as literature. Indeed, they were a part of an important movement of the latter part of the nineteenth century in America, often termed "'the Bible Renaissance,'" to integrate the study of the English Bible as literature into American education and culture (Marsden 241). Perhaps the leading figure in this coordinated effort was William Rainey Harper, the first president of the new University of Chicago, a post he accepted in the early 1890s. As George W. Marsden summarizes in his insightful book, *The Soul of the American University*, however, Harper's interest in elevating the Bible to a central place in American culture started long before arriving at the University of Chicago. He had already become a prominent American promoter of the Bible soon after completing his Ph.D. in ancient languages at Yale in 1875, at the early age of eighteen, and continued to do so with even more zeal and effect, teaching at Denison University, at Morgan Park Theological Seminary, and eventually at Yale University, prior to taking the post at the University of Chicago. His efforts were not limited to higher education, however, since he was one of the leaders of the Chautauqua movement during the 1880s and 1890s, that immensely popular "summer school" for lay people in which the study of the Bible as literature became a central feature (Marsden 240-241). As president of the University of Chicago, Harper wrote these revealing words: "'You understand that my special business in the world is stirring up people on the English Bible. The University of Chicago is entirely a second hand matter'" (quoted in Marsden 241).

What Harper wanted was a new approach to the Bible, different from the Sunday School traditions, an approach that could be a distinguished part of the college curriculum, one that would treat the Bible as a "classic," as taught by "the college teacher of the English Bible" (Wind 103). One of the most important results of Harper's efforts was his ability to influence public universities (the University of Chicago was founded as a Baptist institution) to integrate study of the Bible as literature into their curricula, since such study was not based upon a "religious" approach but on an appreciation of the artistry of the Scriptures (Wind 103). Important to the Seventh-day Adventist heritage is the link Harper established with the University of Michigan in 1893, when one of Harper's students, H. L. Willett, went to Ann Arbor where he became "Chair in English study of the Bible," thus instituting a department which encouraged an approach to the Bible as literature (Wind 103). An early Seventh-day Adventist English teacher, Mahlon Ellsworth Olsen, a former student at Battle Creek College and a disciple of Goodloe Harper Bell, finished his Ph.D. at the University of Michigan in 1909 (Waller, "Some Roots" 132-133). Olsen's degree, the first Ph.D. earned by a Seventh-day Adventist teacher of literature from an American university, had at its core his dissertation entitled *The Evolution of Biblical Prose.*[26] It is not surprising that Olsen would become an important champion of studying the

---

[26]Nearly forty years later, in 1947, Olsen authored a popularized treatment of his dissertation as a book entitled *The Prose of Our King James Version.*

Bible in the literature classroom for the rest of his career as a teacher at Washington Missionary College, at Union College, and as president of the Fireside Correspondence School (forerunner to the Home Study Institute).[27] Another very important link to the establishment of Bible as literature courses throughout the United States, including within Seventh-day Adventist schools, was Professor Richard Green Moulton's series of publications which enhanced such study. Moulton (1849-1924) began as a popular lecturer on English literature in the University of Cambridge's Extension Division, but he was lured by William Rainey Harper to join the faculty of the University of Chicago in 1892, where he eventually became Professor of Literary Theory and Interpretation. Besides being a highly successful lecturer and teacher, Moulton was a prolific author and editor. With Harper's encouragement, he began a series of publications centered on the English Bible as literature. His *The Literary Study of the Bible*, first published in 1895, continued to be reprinted up through 1935. More important, Moulton's *Modern Reader's Bible* was issued first in 1907 and included a definite literary format, with poetry printed in poetic lines and not as verses, along with exhaustive notes and literary commentary (Norton 371-372). This latter text, still being reprinted in the 1950s, became the standard basis for studying the Bible as literature during the first half of the century and was the usual choice by teachers of such courses in Seventh-day Adventist colleges. As David Norton points out, Moulton was in many ways ahead of his time in his approach to literary analysis in general, using a sort of "formalist" approach (see Chapter Two) in order to arrive at conclusions about the genres of Scripture, rather than bogging students down with heavy amounts of historical information and conjectures regarding authorship (373). Perhaps his pioneering approach to the Scriptures was able to live out a long history in literature classrooms of America because of his formalistic assumptions which seemed particularly comfortable when the so-called "New Criticism" gained ascendency from the 1930s to the early 1960s.[28]

---

[27]The most complete research effort on Mahlon Ellsworth Olsen's life and work is contained in John Wesley Taylor V, "Mahlon Ellsworth Olsen: Educational Ideas and Life Sketch," a project paper for a graduate course at Andrews University in 1984.

[28]Inevitably, Moulton's ideas of genre and types in the Scriptures have become outdated, particularly in light of modern biblical scholarship based on archaeological and historical studies which have opened up the understanding of genres and types from the

That the turn-of-the-twentieth-century interest in teaching the Bible as literature affected Seventh-day Adventist teachers of literature can be demonstrated
by noting how early references to a literary approach to the Scriptures entered
the curriculum at Battle Creek College, the first Seventh-day Adventist college in
the United States. The *Battle Creek College Calendar 1896*, for example, specifies that for the Biblical and Literary Course (what today would be termed a
major), students were required to take during the "Senior Year" a year-long
class labeled as "Biblical Literature" (34). In the same publication, a paragraph
description of the "Senior Year" contains this interesting defense of the course:

> The only required work is Biblical Literature in the Bible and Literary
> Course […]. It consists of an examination of the literature having a direct
> bearing upon the sacred Scriptures; as well as a study of the English Bible
> from a literary standpoint. Merely as literature the Bible is properly re-
> garded as the great world-masterpiece, and as such, deserves a thorough
> study from a literary point of view. (15)

The move of Battle Creek College to Berrien Springs, Michigan, in 1901,
included a renaming of the school as Emmanuel Missionary College, but the
traditions about the importance of approaching the Bible as literature survived
the move and became even stronger during the next couple of decades. The
1910-1911 Emmanuel Missionary College Bulletin even credits the work of
the University of Chicago's Professor Richard Green Moulton in its description of the course entitled "Advanced Literature." "One term is given to Biblical Literature, using Moulton's *Introduction to the Literature of the Bible* and
several books in the text of *The Modern Reader's Bible*" (37). By 1919,
Emmanuel Missionary College had again established a separate course for
such study of the Bible, entitled "Biblical Literature," offered for "Four Hours"
of credit over "Eighteen Weeks," described in the following terms:

> The King James and our American Authorized Versions are recognized as
> being worthy of study from the viewpoint of literature. Various books of
> the Bible are studied as masterpieces of literary production. Lectures on
> the types of literature found in the Bible will be given. This course will be
> conducted on the seminar plan and should appeal to many mature stu-
> dents. (*1919-1920 Emmanuel Missionary College Bulletin* 51)

---

ancient periods. Moulton's attempts to explain parts of the Bible in more modern genre
terminology often seem strained, although he is usually relatively flexible in his views, as
noted by Norton (373-376).

Seventh-day Adventists and the Bible as Literature Today

The early emphasis on approaching the Bible as literature in Seventh-day Adventist education has continued throughout the intervening decades. Dr. Wilma McClarty, for example, emphasizes the importance of such an approach in "Why Teach the Bible as Literature?" published in 1989 by the *Journal of Adventist Education*. She underscores the artistic qualities of Bible writings and highlights how an understanding of Bible genres and literary techniques enrich a student's appreciation of Scripture (23+).

A review of the 2000-2001 bulletins of the ten Seventh-day Adventist colleges and universities in the United States and Canada which offer the English major indicates that eight of these institutions continue to have some sort of a course on the Bible as literature as a part of their curricula. What has been at issue, often, however, is whether such a course should be a requirement for all future teachers of literature, as a part of the English major, or whether the course should be an elective. In 1968, responding to criticism about the teaching of modern works which seemed unacceptable in their explicit sexual descriptions and abundance of profanity, North American Division literature teachers, in session at Andrews University, voted a recommendation that all Seventh-day Adventist colleges and universities require a course in the Bible as literature for prospective English teachers.[29] Although that action resulted in moving Bible as literature courses into the required category for English majors at several institutions, not all colleges and universities made such a change, and by 2000-2001, only one college presently requires majors to take such a course. At the other schools, the course is an elective.

Why has there been a turning away from requiring courses in the Bible as literature for English majors in North American Seventh-day Adventist institutions? Certainly one issue has been the recognition that perhaps approaching the Bible as literature should not be the province of teachers of English literature. Are English teachers, non-specialists in the study of the Bible and biblical languages, the best qualified to teach a literary approach to the English Bible? Perhaps not. The last decades of the twentieth century, according to Tremper Longman III, saw an increasing interest among "Biblical scholars," in adapting "the concepts and tools of literary analysis" long

---

[29]Evidently, the participants thought that such an action would somehow reassure their critics about the English major curriculum.

familiar to "literary scholars" to understanding the Scriptures (7). Such an interest inevitably has had an impact on Seventh-day Adventist theologians and biblical scholars as they have done advanced graduate study at Andrews University's Seventh-day Adventist Theological Seminary or other graduate institutions. In the past, when such approaches were the "sole" province of approaches by teachers of literature, such teachers rightly believed that they were adding an important component to the study of Scripture by providing courses in the Bible as literature.[30] More and more often, however, Seventh-day Adventist college, university, and even academy students may meet such literary approaches in Bible classes taught by scholars who have also had required course work in the original biblical languages and other aspects of biblical backgrounds. Such teachers can enrich student understanding of how to interpret from a variety of angles not possible for the traditional teacher of literature.[31]

On the other hand, while one can certainly applaud the influence that literary theory has had on teachers of religion in Seventh-day Adventist courses in biblical study, there are probably still important dimensions which teachers of literature can provide for their majors and other interested students in the Bible as literature courses which are not normally addressed in the same way in religion courses. Literature teachers are particularly well-equipped to uncover the artistry of the Bible, just as they are well-equipped to do so with non-biblical texts. They are also well-versed in modern critical approaches and have often applied such approaches in their own graduate study and publications. They are also less likely than

---

[30]When I took my undergraduate course in Biblical Literature at Pacific Union College as a senior in 1962, for example, I found a way of approaching the Bible that I had never before experienced—one that revitalized my respect for Scripture and one that had specific connection to my approach to other artistic works of literature. Instruction by my professors of biblical study in the required religion courses had not provided this dimension to my appreciation of the Bible, even though they were highly effective in relationship to furthering my understanding of the Seventh-day Adventist perspective on interpreting Scripture.

[31]It is interesting to note that the Bible as literature courses seem to be moving away from English Departments. Union College, the only North American Division institution requiring the course for the English major, offers the course in the Religion Department, presumably taught by a religion teacher. At Walla Walla College, the course is cross-listed in both the English and Religion Departments, with the implication that it may be taught in an interdisciplinary manner or by either a religion teacher or an English teacher.

their colleagues in religion departments to make such literary approaches secondary to doctrinal issues. Such doctrinal issues must be central to the purpose of the required general education religion courses, but there are no such expectations in literature courses where the priorities can be reversed, putting artistic concerns first and doctrinal discussions, *still important, but secondary to and growing out of aesthetic issues.* It would be best, of course, if such literature teachers also had at least adequate background in biblical languages and/or theology.

Another important component to courses in the Bible as literature taught by literature teachers is the opportunity to chart the influence of the Bible on other writers of literature, something particularly marked in the heritage of English-speaking countries from the medieval period to the present. Such an emphasis is beyond the scope of the typical approach by religion teachers. One way of providing for such influence study is to ask students to write research papers on a post-biblical author or literary text which describes the type of Bible influence shown by means of reliance on secondary sources as well as on primary analysis of the selected text.[32]

Approaching the Bible as Literature

Approaches to teaching the Bible as literature have evolved through the decades, also. When initially deemed important in the United States in the latter part of the nineteenth and early part of the twentieth centuries, much emphasis rested on the literary superiority of the handling of the English language in the King James or Authorized Version.[33] Olsen was clearly influenced by this type of emphasis in his dissertation *The Evolution of Biblical Prose* and his later (1947) popularized version of his doctoral research, *The Prose of Our King James Version*, in which he discounts the style of the then

---

[32]It should be noted that Seventh-day Adventist literature majors who go on to advanced graduate study often remark on the advantages their backgrounds in biblical literature and reading of the Bible have given them in identifying biblical allusions and patterns in various literary texts over graduate students educated in more secular settings. Unfortunately, that advantage in biblical sources often is offset by a similar disadvantage in understanding ancient "classical" and "mythological" backgrounds and allusions.

[33]David Norton's *A History of the English Bible as Literature* provides a masterful summary and analysis of how the King James Version dominated literary study of the Bible based on its supposedly purity of style, often somehow connected with near worship of other works issued during the English Renaissance, particularly those by Shakespeare. He rebuts much of such mistaken praise (see 351-352).

new Revised Standard version of the New Testament.[34] But Moulton at the turn of the twentieth century had already downgraded style as a primary issue in teaching the Bible as literature and elevated the study of types and forms as more significant (Norton 372-373). The wide distribution of Moulton's works on the Bible as literature helped to move Seventh-day Adventist educators in the United States away from so-called "AVolatry" (the near worship of the Authorized or King James edition based on its supposed superiority of English style[35]) and towards an approach based upon genres and types. An important contributing force in the United States, interestingly, was the Supreme Court "1963 Bible reading decision" of "*Murray v. Curlett*, 370 U.S. 421" and "*Abington v. Schemp*, 374 U.S. 203" in which the Court attempted to clarify the "legal use of the Bible in public education" (Bracher and Barr, in Barr and Piediscalzi 166-167). That clarification, though excluding the teaching of the Bible as religion, gave specific sanction to "'study'" of "'the Bible'" "'for its literary and historic qualities'" (167).

An outgrowth of this ruling was a new interest in including the Bible as literature in school curricula, from elementary through university. One direct result was the establishment by the University of Indiana of a series of Summer Institutes "On Teaching the Bible as Literature" (1970-1978). These Institutes, besides enrolling numerous prospective teachers of the Bible as literature, resulted in the issuance of a number of publications that applied twentieth-century critical theoretical approaches, particularly formalism (see Chapter Two), to specific parts of the Bible (Bracher and Barr 176-77, 182-84).[36]

Perhaps of even greater importance, however, has been the work of Professor Leland Ryken, longtime teacher of literature at Wheaton College. Influenced by the work of the Canadian literary theorist, Northrop Frye (see Chapter Two on "Structuralism"), Ryken, in the 1970s, began issuing a series of publications concerning a literary approach to the Bible, in which he adapted modern

---

[34]See his chapter on "The Revised Standard Version of the New Testament" (201-34).

[35]See Norton, 400-401, to catch a flavor of the conflict between those committed to AVolatry and those in favor of other versions.

[36]Such publications as *Interpretations of Biblical Narratives*, ed. Kenneth R. R. Gros Louis with James S. Ackerman and Thayer S. Warshaw (1974), *The Bible as/in Literature*, by James S. Ackerman and Thayer S. Warshaw (1976), *An Introduction to New Testament Literature*, ed. Donald Juel with James S. Ackerman and Thayer S. Warshaw (1978), and *Literary Interpretations of Biblical Narratives, Volume II*, ed. Kenneth R. R. Gros Louis with James S. Ackerman (1982) have become excellent resources for instructors at every educational level for courses on the Bible as literature.

understandings of genre, archetypal, and formalistic criticism to the Scriptures. Ryken's commitment to Christianity, together with his clearly elucidated analyses of the literary aspects of the English Bible, made his 1974 *The Bible as Literature* the most important text about the literature of the English Bible for Christian literature teachers since the work of Moulton much earlier in the twentieth century. Most Seventh-day Adventist teachers of Biblical literature in the United States used Ryken's 1974 text while it continued in print. Ryken updated and enlarged his ideas about the Bible as literature in two works presently often used by Seventh-day Adventist teachers: *Words of Delight: A Literary Introduction to the Bible* (1987) on the Old Testament and *Words of Light: A Literary Introduction to the New Testament* (1987) on the New Testament.

Ryken's approach can be illustrated by noting the main divisions of these two works. In *Words of Delight*, for example, Ryken includes sections on "Biblical Narrative," "Biblical Poetry," and "Other Biblical Literary Forms." The general divisions include several subdivisions, however. For example, within the section on "Biblical Narrative," Ryken includes sections on "Hero Stories," "Epic," and "Tragedy," while his section on "Other Biblical Literary Forms" covers "Encomium," "Proverb," "Satire," and "Drama" (7). His *Words of Light* is also organized around types and includes the following divisions: "The Gospels," "The Parables," "The Book of Acts," "The Epistles," "Poetry, Proverb, and Hymn," "Oratory," and "The Book of Revelation" (9-10). Ryken charts his adaptation of Frye's archetypal approach to understanding literature in his "Introduction" to *Words of Delight* (25-29) and bases part of his insistence on the "unity of the Bible" on his idea that such "master images" repeat themselves throughout Scripture (28). Ryken combines his reliance on formalistic, structuralist, and archetypal critical approaches throughout these two books on the Bible as literature as he treats the various portions of Scripture, but this perspective is nicely illustrated in his analysis of "Hero Stories," in *Words of Delight*, in which he applies his theory to the stories of Daniel, Gideon, Esther, and Ruth (107-125). He notes with "the Book of Ruth," for example, that "all the resources of storytelling combine—plot, characterization, setting, word patterns, imagery, archetypes, allusions, dialogue—to produce the total effect," what he terms as "the supreme masterpiece of narrative art in the Bible" (120).[37]

---

[37]Other important resources for the study of the Bible as literature include Northrop Frye's *The Great Code: The Bible and Literature* (1981) and Robert Alter's *The Art of Biblical Narrative* (1981) and *The Art of Biblical Poetry* (1985), as well as *The Literary Guide to the Bible*, edited by Robert Alter and Frank Kermode (1987).

An important issue still facing all teachers of the Bible as literature is what version of the Bible to use. Every Western language has prominent favorites, and English is certainly no exception. Although the Authorized or King James Version was for centuries the best single candidate for use in Biblical literature courses in English, based on its almost legendary status among lovers of Renaissance English style and usage, the late nineteenth and twentieth centuries have seen a proliferation of other translations, generally defended as more accurate and scholarly, and, in some cases, even as more artistic.[38] The Seventh-day Adventist teacher of literature is faced with some difficult choices regarding what Bible version to recommend for students in a course on the Bible as literature. Most twentieth-century English literary scholars rely on recent versions rather than the King James for their chosen versions. Moulton, for example, preferred the English Revised Version (Norton 372), while Ryken relies on the Revised Standard Version for all of his biblical quotations in *Words of Delight* and *Words of Light*, although he does not recommend any single version.

One possible approach is to allow students to choose their individual versions for class purposes, thus allowing for students to enrich class discussions by pointing out differences in wording and style among the various versions used by the class members. There are advantages, however, to encouraging students to choose a version which clearly indicates the poetry of the Bible, printed with indentations related to the structure of Bible poetry rather than simply in relationship to the traditional verse separations as if the poetry were instead prose. For readers in English, the Revised Standard Version includes such structural concerns in its printing of Bible poetry, as does the New English Bible. The *Harper Study Bible*, which uses the Revised Standard Version, but also includes short introductions to each Bible book, as well as extensive explanatory notes and marginal references, is an excellent choice for use in Bible as literature courses.[39]

---

[38]See David Norton's *A History of the English Bible as Literature*, in the chapters on "The Revised Version" (327-357) and "The New English Bible" (430-455), for interesting summations of the give-and-take about the artistry or lack of artistry of modern versions.

[39]Published now, beginning in 1965, by Zondervan Bible Publishers, rather than by Harper and Row.

Should Bible as Literature Courses Be Required?

Even though the Bible as literature has been a central curriculum component in the history of Seventh-day Adventist literature teaching, it is apparent that such may not long be the case unless there is a concerted effort to restore such courses as requirements for literature majors. If, for example, many English majors presently graduating from Seventh-day Adventist institutions in the North American Division are not taking such a course, they will not readily see the importance of carrying on this important tradition. They will not understand how approaching the Bible as literature can enrich their own students' understanding of literary types and forms, or how the artistry of large portions of scripture and an appreciation of that artistry can enhance spiritual experience. It is highly unlikely that they will gain such insights in graduate study, since the study of the Bible as literature is not pervasive in most masters' and doctoral programs. Surely one important step that Seventh-day Adventist literature teachers could take in their commitment to enhancing their students' experience with faith and learning would be to require such a course as a central part of their major curriculum. It may be, however, that such courses would be most effectively taught if they were built around an interdisciplinary approach and could include a literature teacher versed in religion and a religion teacher with a knowledge of literary approaches.

CHAPTER SIX

SEVENTH-DAY ADVENTISTS, LITERARY THEORY, AND LITERARY CRITICISM

Seventh-day Adventists who wrote on literature between World War II through the 1960s concentrated almost obsessively on the statements of Ellen White regarding reading, with particular attention to what she meant by her statements about fiction. In general, with the exception of Professor L. W. Cobb, these writers were able to establish that Ellen White's statements and her own practices allowed for some inclusion of fiction for classroom study. At the same time, teachers of literature continued to teach the Bible as literature as an important and safe component of the curriculum. The 1971 "Guide to the Teaching of Literature in Seventh-day Adventist Schools" underscored the importance of conservative reading choices while at the same time providing the opportunity for literature teachers to turn their attention to other, more global issues related to the study of literature, especially issues of literary theory and criticism.

Seventh-day Adventists and Traditional Moral Criticism: Dr. John O. Waller

All of the writing about literary study, from the work of Professor G. H. Bell through that of Dr. John O. Waller, had been authored with an allegiance to a moral criticism approach to reading (see Chapter Two). Even though much attention had been focused on Ellen White's comments about literature, the studies regarding her comments had clearly underscored that the reading of literature has moral and spiritual dimensions. In general, however, these studies spent little time on theory, concentrating instead on the more immediate task of attempting to clarify how readers should read in the light of Ellen White's counsels.

An important exception to this approach came with the work of Waller, who, while undertaking his study of Ellen White and fiction, also gave considerable thought to the theory of how fiction might best be approached by Christian Seventh-day Adventist readers. His seminal paper on this issue, "Some Eclectically Garnered Reflections Concerning the Moral Criticism of Prose Fiction," was delivered at the 1965 gathering of English teachers at La Sierra College. In this paper, Waller bemoans the inadequacy of Seventh-day Adventist teachers in handling fiction because their education has excluded any serious study of this genre (2). He emphasizes that "truth" is often an appropriate consideration in interpreting fiction, even though many Seventh-day Adventists still associate fiction with untruth (3). After enlarging on the differences between popular and serious fiction (5-6), Waller emphasizes that the serious fiction writer is presenting "not merely a representation of experience, but a judgment about experience" (8-9). Such an approach by a writer is best described "not as an act of creation, but of discovery" (9). And such discovery about life experiences means that "the novel is inextricably involved in moral issues" (12). The serious fiction writer, moreover, "wishes most intensely for you and me to agree with his world view, to adopt his values for our own" (13). As readers of serious fiction, Christian teachers and students, says Waller, must guard against overly identifying with fictional characters, for they must approach such reading without losing "the protective value of criticism" (15-16) and must wrestle with the moral effects of what they are reading (16-17). Waller emphasizes that this moral criticism of reading cannot displace aesthetic concerns but that for the Christian the two must function side by side (17-18).

Waller ends his paper by applying the principles he has been discussing to the Seventh-day Adventist classroom. In order to encourage students to evaluate literature within the context of their Christian values, Waller suggests that a sample work of fiction be approached first by asking "each student [to] write out a paragraph stating what truth claims he thinks the story as a whole implies and upon what evidence he things [sic] so" (20). The writing assignment, then, serves as a foundation for class discussion which attempts to evaluate the story's "truth claims" in relationship to other story types of its time as described by literary historians (21). In essence, what Waller is asking his students to do is to examine the world view presented in the story. His list of questions is revealing: "Is our story typical or better (richer and more subtle) than…its contemporaries? Does it postulate some kind of responsible moral order? If not, is it amorality or immorality, obtrusive or kept in the background?" (21-22). He emphasizes the need of students to understand such tendencies as "sentimentality," as well as such world view concepts as "naturalism" and "existentialism," if they are to adequately judge modern fiction (22).

Beginning Steps towards a Seventh-day Adventist Literary Criticism

At the very end of Waller's paper, "Some Eclectically Garnered Reflections Concerning the Moral Criticism of Prose Fiction," after again emphasizing both the difficulty and challenge of encouraging Christian students to practice moral criticism in relationship to their reading, Waller brings up an interesting vision for the future—"the possibility of a scholarly SDA literary criticism" (25). He does not define what such an approach might be, although he does suggest that it cannot "be the work of any one man" but, instead, must be a collective undertaking, one that can make "Adventist literary study [...] a distinguished profession" (25).

It is significant that Waller sensed a need for a Seventh-day Adventist literary criticism in 1965 just as the New Criticism in the United States was beginning to wane, to be replaced by a series of decades of emphasis on a variety of sometimes competing literary theories and approaches to reading (see Chapter Two). Always interested in literary theory and ever alert to changes in scholarly literary circles, Waller perhaps recognized even at this early date the difficulties Seventh-day Adventists might face in harmonizing their faith and beliefs with some of the premises of recent literary theories.[40]

Dr. Robert Dunn and a Seventh-day Adventist Literary Criticism

An important first step towards the realization of Waller's hope for "a scholarly SDA literary criticism" was Dr. Robert P. Dunn's editing of the *Adventist English Newsletter* in the early 1970s and of a collection of readings, *Seventh-day Adventists on Literature* (1974), a book prepared specifically for courses in religion and literature at Loma Linda University.[41] In the "Introduction" to *Seventh-day Adventists on Literature*, Dunn, whose particular interest has been the intersection of religion and literature, expresses

---

[40]Waller in his retirement year of 1987 shared with me his then-most-recent lecture notes on deconstructionism, when that movement was perhaps at its most influential peak in the United States.

[41]Unfortunately, this anthology of readings was issued in a very limited number of copies and is not easily available.

a goal somewhat similar to Waller's call for a "Seventh-day Adventist literary criticism":

> Now that the Church seems willing to admit that we may read <u>some</u> fiction in our classes it may be that some will say we should read <u>all</u> fiction with no consideration given to its religious or moral views. Let us not take this guarded approval as a license to forget the relation of religion to literature altogether. But let us accept it as an opportunity to construct an even better, a more vital and challenging, program of religion and literature. (9)

Even earlier, however, over three issues of the *Newsletter*, stretching from Fall 1972 through Fall 1973, Dunn attempted to outline a rationale for "A Biblical Basis for English Teaching," the title of the three editorials. Early in the first of the series in Fall 1972, Dunn emphasizes the need to go beyond a "defensive" approach to the reading of literature and the need for "a new direction to define the positive goals we may realize as English teachers" (3). His basic starting point is the premise "that a Christian is a citizen of two worlds, the heavenly and the earthly, and that he holds a dual responsibility to both worlds" (3). Although he recognizes the tension of such an existence, he emphasizes that Christ's example must be our central focus of how such a life can be lived. He uses the introductory verses of the first chapter of John, with the emphasis on Christ as "the Word," as the starting point for his argument. "The Word" as Christ can best be understood in three ways: "the creative, the communicative, and the incarnative" (4). He emphasizes first the creative aspect of existence and centers on how Christian teachers of English can help students understand that creative writers of literature mirror this aspect of Christ as Word. Such teachers and students, moreover, also learn to appreciate how "fine language" and word-making exemplify "the power to create" and are the means humans "seek to order and control our world" while at the same time providing "a reflection of a divine order which words imperfectly represent" (4-5).

Christ as "<u>The Communicative Word</u>" provides us with the mission of telling others about Him. Biblical writers and writers of explicitly Christian literature center on such a task, but what about writers of so-called secular literature? How can such literature be seen as a witness of Divinity? Here Dunn relies on Paul's argument in Romans 1 that all of humanity has a revelation "of God in nature"; thus, as Paul's experience in Athens illustrates, so-called pagan writers provide glimpses of truth. Literature teachers, then, have a responsibility to share with their students "the best secular literature" through which "a reader may feel the power of the Holy Spirit and catch a glimpse of the divine order" (5).

Most important, however, is seeing Christ as "The Incarnative Word," for it is Christ as Man and God that links together the human aspects of Christ as "Creative Word" and the divine aspects of Christ as the "Communicative Word," thus providing for humanity a full vision of how human beings, with Divine help, can live in this world as well as the world to come. In an interesting analogy, Dunn suggests that poetry's ability to join history and philosophy in order to reveal truth is similar to Christ's joining of Divinity with humanity in order also to reveal truth. He emphasizes that how human beings respond to the story of Christ's life and death is mirrored, however imperfectly, in the human responses to works of literature. This is not to say that literature is a method of "evangelism" or a way to win "converts" (6). But what literature can do is to provide "a vision of the world, and the greater the literature, the closer it will approximate the true order of the world, the order revealed by the Word" (6).

In the second of his editorials, Winter-Spring 1973, Dunn continues his theoretical outline. Here, he is concerned with charting a middle ground between two types of literature teachers: those who believe that "we should read as little of this kind of literature [secular literature] as possible" and those who do not want to see artificial connections made between secular literature and spiritual issues (3). Dunn's middle ground, one that provides for the integration of faith with the teaching of literature, rests on his view of how grace exists in the midst of human depravity. Secular literature, thus, can reveal the truth about God and human experience, if read in its largest implications and if approached with the truth of God's grace as allowing for glimpses of such truth amid a world characterized by evil. He blames the New Criticism for shaping some Seventh-day Adventist teachers of literature in their attitudes that religion and morality should be separated from approaches to literature. He insists that such thinking is now (in 1973) becoming outdated, as evidenced by the explosion of approaches that seek interdisciplinary links between the arts and "science," "psychology," "politics," as well as "religion" (6). He concludes by stating that "all serious literature…is religious in the root sense of the term," meaning the desire "'to bind together again' man's faith […]'" (6).

In the final part of his editorial series, Fall 1973, Dunn turns his attention to how a study of apocalypse would be particularly relevant to the Seventh-day

Adventist literature classroom. He emphasizes how the church's emphasis on Christ's "Second Advent" naturally gives itself to thinking about the end of the world and the hope of a new world (3). He believes that the study of the genre of apocalypse can help Adventist students to understand better the tension which exists from living fully in this world while looking forward to the world that is coming. Besides studying the biblical books of Daniel and Revelation in such a course, students would also study more recent examples of apocalypse. Such an approach will lead students to better estimate their own false reliance on materialism and better appreciate how "the apocalyptic vision" in both biblical and non-biblical writers grows out of a "sense of world-weariness" (5). His hope is that this type of study will lead students to find a balance between life in this world and the life to come. He ends his series by insisting that "we English teachers must do more to help our students discover meaning for their lives. And since for us meaning is ultimately religious, we cannot avoid dipping into religion, however imperfectly at first" (6).

Dunn began building on his *Newsletter* editorials in his anthology, *Seventh-day Adventists on Literature,* with an essay entitled "The Image of Faith in Literature and Life" (175-193). At the beginning of this essay, Dunn emphasizes that his will not be an "apologetic approach" which attempts to answer "critics who would too narrowly restrict the range of the Christian's reading," but rather he will attempt to address "the positive role that literature may legitimately play in the Christian life" (175). He does so by specifically explaining how for Seventh-day Adventists literature and religion can be properly related. Dunn suggests that of models sketched in H. Richard Niebuhr's *Christ and Culture,* Seventh-day Adventists fit best into the "'Christ and Culture in Paradox'" paradigm (179), a mode of operation that "'requires obedience to the institutions of society and loyalty to its members as well as obedience to a Christ who sits in judgment on that society'" (178). The result is a constant tension that reveals itself in the Seventh-day Adventist paradox of attempting "to remain loyal to God above all, but in such a way as to fulfill their obligations to society" (179). In spite of this tension, culture and the works of culture remain important to the Christian, and the "Christian teacher will ask [...] how literature, which is a specific cultural activity, may be related to faith, which although it operates within the context of culture finally transcends the realm of the human" (181).

Dunn turns to Sallie TeSelle's *Literature and the Christian Life* for a guide to this integration of literature study with Christian faith. He suggests that her sketch of the "'theological criticism'" of literature is to him a very attractive approach because "its purpose is not to judge orthodoxy in literature, not to make literature a tool for the theologian in his theological work, but to examine, as objectively as possible, the kinds of faith represented in literature" (182). This approach to understanding literature has direct bearing on "the Christian life" and is, therefore, preferable to approaches which are more limited in their results (183).

Dunn's attempt to explain how "theological criticism" works, however, is somewhat obscure as he elaborates on the differences between "'calculative thinking,'" "'existential'" thinking, and "'primordial'" or "'essential thinking'" (184-185), even though he indicates that the last of these forms of thinking (the "primordial") provides the reader of literature with the fullest and richest spiritual experience as a result of reading literature. Although not always clear in his efforts, Dunn's wide-ranging attempt to underscore how analogy, symbol, and myth relate to spiritual development is a refreshing change from the usual Seventh-day Adventist preoccupation with interpreting Ellen White's counsels on appropriate reading.

Language Matters: *Another Step Towards a Seventh-day Adventist Literary Criticism*

Waller's call for a "a collective undertaking" in Seventh-day Adventist literary criticism came closer to fulfillment as a result of yet another meeting of educators, the North American Division Higher Education Council at Andrews University in 1976. At that meeting, the English teachers hearkened to the concerns of Dr. Ottilie Stafford, chair of the English Department at Atlantic Union College, and determined to produce a book about English as a discipline for the Seventh-day Adventist audience. Two years later, in 1978, after several meetings of the committee of writers who produced the manuscript, the volume *Language Matters: Notes Toward an Adventist English Program*, under the general editorship of Dr. Verne Wehtje of Pacific Union College, was published by the Southern Publishing Association.

One of the main motives for the book was a concern that the forces calling for a movement "back to the basics" within society and within the denomination might narrow the educational focus for English and language arts teachers to an unbalanced concentration on grammar, mechanics, and utilitarian writing. The teachers at the 1976 meetings felt their discipline had been misunderstood all too often and needed a coherent explanation. As the "Preface" to *Language Matters,* by Verne Wehtje, indicates: "If there is no clear understanding of the place of English in Adventist schools, can we speak to the issues in such a way that our understanding will be clarified and sharpened and that our work will be improved?" (5).

The various chapters in the book were authored by eight different teachers of English and communication. Since the book was intended to provide a holistic overview of English as a discipline, literature study was not the single central focus of the volume, although Dunn authored a specific chapter on literature, entitled "Twin Tasks of the English Teacher" (87-109). Other writers, however, touched on the importance of literature study for the Christian student as they developed chapters primarily devoted to other areas of the discipline.

In her overview introductory chapter, "At the Center of Development," Ottilie Stafford, for example, provides a rather far-reaching and complete theoretical, albeit brief, justification for the Christian Seventh-day Adventist study of literature. Stafford's emphasis on the moral and spiritual development of students is tied first to language study. She uses an Ellen White quotation as her entrance into her discussion: "'More important than the acquirement of foreign languages, living or dead, is the ability to write and speak one's mother tongue with ease and accuracy; but no training gained through a knowledge of grammatical rules can compare in importance with the study of language from a higher point of view. With this study, to a great degree, is bound up life's weal or woe'" (9). Stafford then emphasizes that character and moral development are intricately tied to language development, since "language and thought are inextricably intertwined [...]" (10). For Christians, "language development" and "development of moral understanding are seen as simultaneous processess" (10).

Stafford charts three main levels of language study: the utilitarian, the metaphoric, and the symbolic. It is the two latter levels of language study which relate specifically to the importance of literature for Christian study. Addressing the metaphoric use of language, Stafford notes that language on this "deeper level" affects "the emotions as well as the mind, and [is] closely linked to personality development [...]" (14). She emphasizes "that metaphor is the basis of most Biblical statement" and, as such, forms the foundation for a person's "commitment to Christian belief [...]" (14). Language facility with metaphor is grounded in "the study of poetry" and "other creative forms of writing," those forms which historically have been the center of literature courses (15). She insists that teachers "who feel comfortable teaching grammar, but do not like poetry, ought not to be in Christian English classrooms, for they will limit the ability of their students to experience and to express the feelings and thoughts that are at the center of Christian experience" (15). An even deeper level of language facility than the metaphoric, however, is the symbolic.

Says Stafford, "There is something that lies deep in the human nature that recognizes symbols as a way of getting at the central meanings of life" (15). She cites the Book of Revelation as an example of the richness of "symbolic structures" which allow us "to understand much more than theological statements could express [...]" (15). "The adult and critical reader" comes to see how the symbolic uses of language function most completely and deeply through the study of such literature (15-16). "The English program the Christian teacher directs should center in the language development of the individual, with work in the basic structures of language, oral and written composition, and rich and varied selections of literature, with much emphasis on poetry and other metaphoric forms" (16).

Robert Dunn's chapter on literature in *Language Matters*, "Twin Tasks of the English Teacher," is a much clearer statement of how literature study can be linked to spiritual development than his earlier essay in *Seventh-day Adventists on Literature* had been. The "Twin Tasks" of the title refer to the paradox of Seventh-day Adventist Christian development—the need to prepare for Christ's soon return and life in eternity on the one hand, while at the same time encouraging individuals to live full lives in this world, following the pattern of Christ. Dunn emphasizes that both "Tasks" are important to the literature teacher, even though "conference administrators and sometimes school administrators, parents, teachers, and students feel that the primary task of the School is to prepare students for heaven and that personal or social adjustment is secondary or trivial" (88).

Dunn distinguishes three stages in literary development—the "aesthetic," the "ethical," and the "spiritual" (88)—although he admits that these stages often co-exist and overlap in a classroom of students or in a community. He emphasizes that the aesthetic stage "preeminently characterizes the early years of a young child's life or the first periods of growth of a civilization" (89). Children in this state of literary development revel in the sounds of words and the rhythms and rimes of poetry; they "delight in language" (90). Even so, however, this aesthetic stage also includes a beginning development of "ethical and spiritual awareness" (90). It is important in this stage, however, not to overemphasize "moral, religious, or philosophical meaning" of literary works, but instead to nurture this childhood "delight in spiritual experience," since all too often such delight is erased by an overemphasis on the seriousness of the moral and spiritual dimensions of what is read (91-93). Dunn associates the "aesthetic" stage with Greek civilization (94-95).

The second stage of literary development, "ethical awareness," is that phase in which "there is a growing tendency to see community joined by a sense of a law that stands over against and judges the community or person" (96). Dunn associates this stage particularly with "the high school years" and underscores how important it is that "a connection be made between aesthetic beauty and moral beauty" (96). In this stage, emphasis should be placed on values, and teachers would do well to choose literary works that address the growing concerns of young people about how to behave in society (97-98). Dunn associates the ethical phase of development with Hebrew culture and indicates that the Bible can be used to reinforce student awareness of the inevitable task of dealing ethically with one another (99-101).

The final stage of literary development, "spiritual awareness," includes "the first two moments of aesthetic and ethical consciousness, but it goes beyond these stages to apprehend a form of beauty that can neither be perceived by the senses nor that is centered primarily in social ends" (101). But spiritual awareness "is the gift of God," and, therefore, presents a quandary for the literature teacher, for how does one encourage students to develop what is provided by divine grace (102-103)? The first requirement is that the teacher must have "experienced something of this spiritual vision" (103). For the Seventh-day Adventist, however, there are other encouragements towards the development of spiritual awareness in students. Teachers can reveal the "Twin Tasks" of their belief system—their understanding of Christ's love as revealed in the paradox of His soon coming kingdom and His desire that we live fully in this world until He comes. The literature teacher has a special opportunity to emphasize how these "Twin Tasks" are really one and the same. Literature teachers are especially prepared to handle such seeming paradoxes and ironies, and are well able "to work back and forth between biblical and secular literature," as they explore how irony pervades all of life and is revealed in literary study (105-108). Such an approach, however, does not mean "that every piece of literature read should be compared with the Bible or given a spiritual application" (108). But since usually students take no more than "one literature class in college," it seems unfortunate for them to graduate, having learned "much about literary form and style, much about a particular author or period, but little of [...] [their] own spiritual heritage" (108).

Seventh-day Adventists and Recent Literary Theory: Dr. Douglas Jones and Dr. Daniel Reynaud

Although literary theory has been central to the study of literature in the Western World during the past fifty years and has become a particularly controversial area in the United States, few Seventh-day Adventists have directly addressed how the Christian should relate to recent literary theories. Dr. Douglas Jones, however, in an article entitled "Why Study Literature?" published in *The Journal of Adventist Education* in 1989, emphasizes that reader-response approaches (see Chapter Two) can be successfully linked to the moral and spiritual emphasis that Seventh-day Adventist teachers of literature have long valued. Directing his article at secondary school teachers of literature, Jones notes that "we [teachers of literature] need to share with our students the ways literature helps us to gain insight into the human condition, into morality and values" (19). Jones asserts that the best way of involving students in literature study is through adopting the techniques of reader-response theory. He briefly traces Louise Rosenblatt's theory that "literature exists as performance," that is, how the "interaction" of "the reader and the ink marks (the text)" results in a "transaction" that actually creates the work of literature. "The end product is composed by the author's creativity and intention, colored by the personality, intentions and experiences of the reader" (20).

Jones ends his article by briefly describing how reader-response theory can be implemented in the classroom. He notes that using such an approach means "a shift from emphasizing the 'meaning' of the poem, or the author's meaning in the poem, to what the poem means to the student […]" (20). Students should be allowed to express their responses without fear of being judged right or wrong. The teacher in such a classroom is not "the all-knowing dispenser of answers, the last word," but instead functions as a guide to help students in their discoveries (20). Background lectures about literature and authors should be dispensed with as much as possible and replaced by class activities that "help teenagers to bring their experiences to the text and then participate in the *poem*" (21). In particular, students should be allowed to "choose their own reading" as much as possible, with the teacher attempting to "balance the literary diet in our classrooms between a variety of self-selected works and occasional classics" (21). Jones admits that the reader-response approach may be offensive to some because it seems not to conform to "back-to-basics" concerns; however, what needs to be remembered is that the really important matters for the literature classroom are the goals of "fostering understanding and compassion, developing judgment, exploring attitudes and ethics" (21, 42).

Dr. Daniel Reynaud presents an ambitious attempt to assess how contemporary literary theory relates to Christianity and, specifically, the Seventh-day Adventist faith in his article in *Spectrum*, entitled "Secular Theory and Religious Faith: How to Think Christian in a Postmodern Society," published in 2000.[42] Reynaud categorizes three general approaches to literature: (1) "the traditional author-centered approach" in which the author is seen as the best authority on meaning in a text; (2) "textual approaches" (including the "Formalists, Structuralists, Semioticians, and Marxists") for which the "text" and the "context" provide the best entrance into meaning; and (3) "Postmodernism" in which the "reader" becomes paramount in establishing a kind of relative and tentative meaning (6-9). (See Chapter Two for brief explanations of these approaches.) In his essay, Reynaud is concerned to emphasize how the various approaches affect one's understanding of the Bible and how all literary approaches have strengths as well as weaknesses. He notes that the "author-centered" approach is most comfortable for those who believe that "God is the author of the Bible" and that the "Christian's task is simply to read what the Bible says and then to accept that as God's word, true, universal, and unchangeable" (6). But such a position is really not compatible with those parts of the Bible which are not "transparent" (6). Moreover, a belief in "verbal inspiration" (that God as author dictated the Bible) is something that Seventh-day Adventism has never accepted. Text-centered approaches also have weaknesses when applied to the Bible; however helpful in "unraveling various sources from which the existing text [...] was compiled, and in identifying literary genres," they can lead traditional Christians to doubt "the divine inspiration of the Bible" (6).

Very importantly, Reynaud addresses "Postmodernism" in the latter parts of his essay. He links "deconstructionism and reader-response" theory (see Chapter Two), emphasizing that placing the reader as determinant in establishing meaning leads inevitably to relativism. With such contemporary

---

[42]Reynaud's essay was written as a part of the Twenty-Second International Faith and Learning Seminar, held in 1998, and appeared in its first version as "Literary Theory and Biblical Interpretation," *Christ in the Classroom: Adventist Approaches to the Integration of Faith and Learning*, compiled by Humberto Rasi, vol. 21 (Silver Spring, MD: Institute for Christian Faith, 1998), 279-92.

theories, there can be "no universal truth" for "each reader constructs her own truth, according to her set of experiences and the parameters of the text." Such "a view presents that greatest contemporary challenge to the Christian," for it "deconstructs the very foundations of Christianity, removing the authority of the Bible as the revealed Word of God and reducing it merely to a series of constructs made by individual readers" (8).

But, at the same time, postmodernism provides some valuable insights into reality, argues Reynaud. It underscores the variability of meaning and language, the relativity of human experience. "Their [postmodernists'] relativist ideas are undeniably true when applied to humanity, providing an excellent explanation of the human world. It is true that we are relative beings, imperfect, incapable of grasping the universal, always understanding and expressing it in incomplete, imperfect terms" (9). Even so, however, postmodern theory is not a completely convincing approach to understanding meaning. No matter how "slippery" language may be or how variable readers' meanings may turn out, human beings still manage "to achieve significant consensus on meaning. Cultural and literary contexts contribute a pool of common codes that constrain the meanings of texts. Genres help readers determine the nature of meaning [...]. Authors are involved in shaping meaning by their choice of genre and their skill in manipulating language" (9).

Reynaud's "Christian Model" for approaching meaning is informed by the three categories he has established: author-centered approaches, text-centered approaches, and postmodernism. He emphasizes that God is in a sense the "author" of the Bible and is "absolute, perfect." The Bible (the text) is a "meeting point of absolute and relative, perfect and imperfect," since it is the result of a mixture of human and divine authorship. The reader ["me"] is always "relative, imperfect," thus, parallel to the emphasis of postmodernism (9). Adopting the best from the three categories of literary approaches clarifies the dilemma of the Seventh-day Adventist Christian in approaching the Scriptures. The acceptance of the reality that the text and the reader are to some extent imperfect in their representations of the divine and of truth can save the Seventh-day Adventist believer from "dogmatism, pride, and a persecuting attitude toward those who differ from us" while at the same time allowing for "a secure base from which to face challenges to our faith" (10). The model allows us to see that the problems in seeing the truth of the divine lies not in the author of truth (God) or even in the text (the Bible), although some imperfections may be inherent in non-verbal inspiration, but rather in ourselves, for "it is not God who is inadequate; it is our understanding of him" (10).

Reynaud's essay is the most direct and thoughtful attempt written by a Seventh-day Adventist to wrestle with contemporary theory. It is particularly helpful in its effort to relate such theory to the reading of the Scriptures. Unlike many conservative Christians, Reynaud refuses to provide a blanket condemnation of Postmodernism, but instead finds some strengths in deconstructionism and reader-response theory, while at the same time recognizing the essential hostility of the basic assumptions of such approaches to central Christian and Seventh-day Adventist beliefs. But, of course, what Reynaud's essay does not do is to relate contemporary literary theory to non-biblical literary texts. He has left it up to others to adapt his model for approaching Scripture to other works of literature.

Other Recent Writing by Seventh-day Adventists on Literature and Literary Theory

The 1978 *Language Matters: Notes Toward an English Program* marked a high point in Seventh-day Adventist attempts to develop a theoretical basis for the study of literature. Since the book was a group effort, it also came close to fulfilling Dr. John O. Waller's earlier call for "a concerted effort" to establish a "Seventh-day Adventist literary criticism." In truth, the last two decades have not seen any *concerted advance* among literature teachers in their writing about the theory of the relationship between faith and literary theory beyond the contents of this important publication (the articles by Jones and Reynaud are exceptions).

Instead, literature teachers have devoted their efforts to rather specific applications of their Christian faith to particular literary works or to specific continuing problems related to Seventh-day Adventist concerns about literature. Such approaches have been enhanced by the regular International Faith and Learning Seminars, sponsored by the Education Department of the General Conference of Seventh-day Adventists, beginning in 1988. Seventh-day Adventist literature teachers have participated regularly in such seminars, but in general have been unwilling to tackle large, overriding issues of theory, preferring instead to illustrate how Christian faith and learning can be integrated in the Seventh-day Adventist classroom by means of concentration on a specific author or work of literature.[43]

---

[43]See, for example, Gatsinzi Basaninyenzi's "Teaching an Anti-Christian Text from a Christian Perspective: The Case of S. Beckett's *Waiting for Godot*," or Iris Henry's "Teaching

An important exception to this type of text- or author-centered focus from participants in the International Faith and Learning Seminars is the more recent essay by Southern Adventist University's Dr. Jan Haluska, entitled "The Bible and Literature," published in 2000. Haluska's article is an ambitious and wide-ranging attempt to establish a Christian and Seventh-day Adventist approach to literature based on biblical principles and precedents.[44] Early in his writing, Haluska redefines his title, suggesting that "'The Bible Versus Other Kinds of Literature' might be a better choice" (365-66). What follows in his essay is a brief survey of attitudes towards literature as displayed by the various phases of Bible writing and writing about the Bible: the "Old Testament" first, then the "New Testament," then writers about the Bible during "the last two thousand years," and, finally, writing of our own time, "especially seen with the guidance of Ellen G. White" (366).

Doubtless, such a survey approach is too ambitious for the number of pages provided in the essay. More depth regarding each phase would enrich the persuasiveness of the conclusions reached. Regardless, the essay is highly suggestive and quite valuable in its insights. Haluska is at pains to point out that neither the Old or New Testament writers of the Bible actually condemn so-called pagan literature of their own contemporary cultures, no matter how hostile such cultures seem to have been to biblical principles (380). In his coverage of post-biblical writers about Scripture and literature, Haluska fairly admits the various attitudes of Church fathers such as Tertullian and Augustine (generally negative towards secular literature) and Justin, Origen, and Clement (somewhat positive towards the same literature) (380-84). Similarly, the church fathers of the later middle ages as well as Protestant leaders of the Reformation displayed similar inconsistencies in their various stances regarding the value of secular literature, with the Puritans being, for example, less uniform in their proscriptions regarding drama than has generally been recognized (384-87). Haluska's quick trip through early Seventh-day Adventist thinking regarding literature is highly reliant on the stance of Ellen White as seen by Waller (387-90). He concludes that Mrs. White was "far more proscriptive" in her stance than most writers before "Tertullian, Minucius Felix, or Augustine," but he also notes balancing

---

Shakespeare within the Context of Christian Faith: A Case Study of *Macbeth*," or Carol Sample's "The Salvation Theme in Flannery O'Connor."

[44]Haluska does not really address contemporary literary theory, however.

quotations from her writing that underscore the importance of "'literary training'" (389). Thus, argues Haluska, "God's remnant people are to avoid the impure, but not to be so afraid of contact with the world's literature that we adopt a siege mentality" (390).

Perhaps the most important parts of Haluska's essay are the last sections, however, in which he attempts briefly to chart how the Seventh-day Adventist teacher of literature goes about "Teaching Literature Positively" and "Teaching Literature Negatively" (393-99). Using as his examples Chaucer's Parson from *The Canterbury Tales* and Homer's *Iliad*, Haluska demonstrates how the literature teacher can lead students to appreciate both an explicitly Christian text as well as a pagan text when both are approached positively from the perspective of a balanced Christian world view. Similarly, a negative approach to a work of literature (in this case, Plato's *Apology of Socrates*), pointing out the limitations and prejudices of Plato's exoneration of Socrates as clarified by matching it with the more negative picture of Socrates presented by Xenophon in his *Socrates Defense to the Jury*, helps students understand that regardless of the beauty and persuasiveness of Plato's writing, his world view is antagonistic to a Christian perspective and his ennobling of Socrates has too easily tempted generations of Christian readers to elevate Socrates to the level of Christ (396-99).

Haluska ends his brief journey through the ages of Bible writing and writing about the Bible with a ringing call for "Christian English teachers" to be willing "to guide their students appropriately through the most powerful non-biblical books in history. Scripture allows it, and although post-New Testament writings and Mrs. White's counsels are cautionary, they too sanction it" (399).

Seventh-day Adventists and Literary Theory: Directions for the Future

When one reviews the writings of Seventh-day Adventists about literature and literary theory, as I have done in preparing this manuscript, one has to admit that most of the contributions have been reactive and apologetic rather than proactive and ground-breaking in their attempts to provide a basis for approaching literature from a Seventh-day Adventist perspective. Writers have reacted first to the statements of Ellen White, attempting to clarify such statements and find some sort of balanced approach to reading that would allow for the study of some fiction and drama, genres much emphasized in the modern literature classroom. Even the attempts to initiate a sort of Seventh-day Adventist literary criticism have generally been framed within the work of other Christian or "moral" theorists about literature and the arts.[45]

It should be recognized that Seventh-day Adventists are not the only Christians who have had difficulty in devising a distinct literary criticism. As Leland Ryken has pointed out, modern Christians in general have not been particularly adept in mounting a unique "Christian criticism," although the hostility of certain modern literary theories to basic Christian premises demands the formation of Christian literary theory (Ryken, "Afterword" 297-98). But Ryken goes ahead to underscore that "an aesthetic based on the broad foundation of Christian doctrine will intersect at virtually every turn with critical traditions from Aristotle through the latest critical fashion" (299). One can assume, then, that a Seventh-day Adventist theory of literature, should one develop, will also be heavily reliant on the "critical traditions" of past and present, just as Seventh-day Adventist theology is similarly dependent on such traditions and frameworks. Ryken recognizes that some contemporary Christian writers about literature have at least accomplished "half of the task of Christian literary theory" in that they have reacted to current literary criticism, but they have not yet been able "to develop a Christian aesthetic based on principles derived from the Christian critic's own agenda of interests, including Christian doctrine" ("Afterword" 300-01).[46] What

---

[45]Dr. John O. Waller relies on a variety of nineteenth- and twentieth-century Christian literary critics in his "Some Eclectically Garnered Reflections Concerning the Moral Criticism of Prose Fiction." And Dr. Douglas Jones and Daniel Reynaud react to various modern literary theories from a Seventh-day Adventist perspective in their articles "Why Study Literature?" and "Secular Theory and Religious Faith: How to Think Christian in a Postmodern Society," rather than setting up a consistent Seventh-day Adventist theoretical model for approaching literary study, although Reynaud does set up a model for approaching Scripture which might be adapted to secular literature. Jan Haluska's essay, though wide-ranging in its attempt to see literature from a biblical perspective, really is concerned more with what the Bible writers and writers about the Bible actually say about the reading of non-biblical literature than about establishing literary theory based on biblical theological principles.

[46]Perhaps the best book I have found that fulfills Ryken's desire for a work which links reactions to contemporary literary theory to an examination of literature from a Christian perspective is *People of the Book: Christian Identity and Literary Culture*, by David Lyle Jeffrey. In this text, Jeffrey emphasizes how certain contemporary theorists have misunderstood how traditional Christianity has regarded texts and language, and, concentrating on specific authors and works, he traces how Christianity has been a beneficial and important foundation for literature throughout English literary history, including the twentieth century.

Ryken asserts about Christian literary theory in general can certainly be applied to Seventh-day Adventist writers about literature. Such writers have
generally reacted to criticism of their discipline by Seventh-day Adventist
leaders and readers. Their writing about literature prior to the 1970s was
heavily dependent on explaining the comments of Ellen White. The publication of *Language Matters: Notes Toward an English Program* in 1978 laid a
foundation for future publications regarding an Adventist literary theory. But
in the last two decades of the twentieth century, after the initial steps made
in the 1970s, few Seventh-day Adventist teachers of literature have attempted
to build on those foundations.

Some might well argue that Seventh-day Adventist teachers of and writers about literature would be better off contributing to the general formation of
a Christian literary criticism, called for by Ryken, rather than narrowly concentrating on the relationship of their own unique theology to literature. Such
a more general Christian emphasis makes sense when one remembers that
Seventh-day Adventism holds much more in common with Christianity's general belief system than it holds separately or uniquely. As Dr. Fritz Guy notes
in his book *Thinking Theologically: Adventist Christianity and the Interpretation of Faith*, "For to be Adventist is to be, first and foremost, Christian; and
what is most important in Adventist experience, practice, and belief is not
what differentiates us from other Christians but what unites us to them" (ix).

On the other hand, most Seventh-day Adventists would certainly see
their belief system as somehow unique and special, differing in important
ways from the doctrines and practices of other Christian denominations.
Just what is this uniqueness, then, and how can this distinctiveness be used
by Seventh-day Adventist teachers of literature as a starting point for the
development of a Seventh-day Adventist theory of literature? What follows
are some thoughts on what directions such an approach might take.

Seventh-day Adventist Theology and Literary Theory

It is not so much any single belief or practice that characterizes Seventh-
day Adventism as it is a composite emphasis on certain beliefs and practices that distinguishes Adventism from other Christian belief systems.
Seventh-day Adventism, for example, has at its core the widely held
Christian focus on the gospel and its related implications as central lynch
pins of its theology. Thus, Adventism embraces God's existence and His
"everlasting, universal, and comprehensive love" as its most
basic and comprehensive pillar (Guy 229). The gospel's picture of how

God's love provides for victory over sin and salvation through Christ's death and the gospel's promise of reconciliation and eternal life lived in the presence of a loving God undergird the hope of every Seventh-day Adventist Christian believer. Any Seventh-day Adventist literary theory must begin with such more generally-held Christian premises, then, and include what Ryken has called "an Aesthetic based on the broad foundation of Christian doctrine [...]" ("Afterword" 299). That "broad foundation" would include such various intersecting Christian doctrines which radiate from the gospel and its emphasis on God's love as belief in "Scripture or special revelation," as well as belief in "common grace and natural revelation," the latter two being very central to a Christian literary theory in that they "assert that all truth is God's truth and that we do not need to inquire into the Christian orthodoxy of writers before we know whether they have spoken the truth" (299-300).[47]

But what about that particular Seventh-day Adventist theological perspective, those unique emphases within Christian theology, which should be a part of any Seventh-day Adventist literary criticism? Building on the general Christian centrality of the gospel's picture of God's love, Seventh-day Adventists have established their identity around the following doctrines and emphases, none of which are singular, but which taken together form a distinctiveness that separates Adventism from other Christian bodies. These theological elements that characterize the "distinctive Adventist heritage," Fritz Guy summarizes as the "Sabbath," the "Advent hope, the continuing ministry of Christ, human wholeness, and truth" (237).

What is most important about such a list of Seventh-day Adventist beliefs as far as literary theory is concerned is to realize their fundamental implications rather than simplifying them into a list of dos and don'ts about reading. That is, it would be a mistake to assume that readers should not read imaginative works which contradict Adventist beliefs about which day is the Sabbath or which ignore Christ's continuing redeeming work in the heavenly sanctuary. Although such prohibitions would certainly simplify reading choices to a very few works outside of the Bible, they would also

---

[47]To attempt to elaborate a complete Christian view of literary theory would go beyond the purposes of this present study. The reader is referred to Clarence Walhout and Leland Ryken, eds., *Contemporary Literary Theory: A Christian Appaisal*, for an introduction that helps to get one thinking.

contradict the basic general Christian gospel doctrine of common grace which accepts that "all truth is God's truth," that in all human endeavor truth exists, albeit alongside falsehood or imperfections. When looked at in some depth, each of the pillars of the Adventist heritage, as emphasized by Fritz Guy, reveals implications about God's loving character and appropriate human responses to that character which go far beyond a kind of surface allegiance to their belief requirements. The Sabbath, for example, functions as a "'seal' of our relationship to God and thus an experience of the meaning of our humanness" (237). As such, it is also a reminder that God acts in relationship to time in His love for humanity, an indication of "spiritual freedom" from "routine obligations," "a symbol through which we can reflect on and experience the presence of ultimacy in our human existence," and even a recognition of "human dignity, equality, and justice" since it provides for each "person" to be "related directly to God" without "hierarchies of status" (238-40).[48] Similarly, the Sanctuary doctrine's emphasis on Christ's continuing ministry in heaven is best seen as an indication of God's continued presence in our lives, His continuing interest in our salvation, and His nearness and immanence, for "God has not retired from the process of atonement" (244). The "Advent hope" regarding Christ's soon return is fundamentally a *"hope in the ultimate triumph of God's love"* (240); the Adventist emphasis on human wholeness (the health message) underscores God's desire for humans to recognize that God participates "in all of the dimensions of humanness," that there "is a unity of body and mind (and/or spirit)," and that God values all aspects of human health, including sexuality and diet (246-49). The Adventist heritage of *"commitment to truth"* in its broadest sense is a recognition of the "ultimacy of God" and "living accordingly," even though human perception of truth is necessarily "never more than an approximation" (249-250).

A Seventh-day Adventist literary criticism, then, would take these fundamental Adventist principles in their broadest gospel implications as the conscious basis for approaching literature. God's character and love as divulged in the Scriptures would be central to building such a criticism, but the Adventist emphases that grow out of that central focus would characterize a Seventh-day Adventist literary theory. In the past, most Seventh-day

---

[48]I have only touched on a few of the implications of the Sabbath and the other Seventh-day Adventist characteristic doctrines as noted by Guy.

Adventist (and, in truth, most Christian) writers about literature have not explicitly used basic gospel premises as their starting point for their writing about literature. In the case of Seventh-day Adventist teachers of literature, much of their effort has gone into clarifying and contextualizing the comments of Ellen White about reading and literature, since these comments have been most often the central focus of church leaders and members. Inevitably, the writing that has grown out of these efforts has been largely apologetic, attempting to carve out a place for literary study in spite of Ellen White's prohibitions. What is now needed, if a Seventh-day Adventist literary criticism is to develop, is for Seventh-day Adventist teachers of and writers about literature to do conscious thinking and writing about how the gospel in its multifaceted dimensions can form the basis of a Christian Seventh-day Adventist approach to literature.

In a sense, Dr. Robert Dunn has come closer than any other Seventh-day Adventist writer to the development of such an approach when he traced a rationale for literature teaching based on his analysis of Christ as "The Word," along with his emphasis upon the relationship between grace and depravity in the present world and his concern with how the study of apocalypse can help students better understand the tensions of living in the present world while preparing for life in the future world (see the editorials summarized above in this chapter). Dunn also addresses the "nature of Christian spirituality" in the last section of his chapter on the "Twin Tasks of the English Teacher" in *Language Matters*, published in 1978 (see the separate section on this book earlier in this chapter). Not only does Dunn center on the central doctrine of God's love, but he also emphasizes the "radical," "eschatological" aspect of that love, thus linking the Seventh-day Adventist concern with hope for the future with the necessity of living in the present (103-04). Interestingly, in the first part of his editorial series in the *Adventist English Newsletter*, Dunn recognized that it would be impossible for him "to outline a complete rationale" for a Seventh-day Adventist approach to literature. Such a comprehensive Seventh-day Adventist literary theory would need "to be accomplished by a representative group, not by one person" (3). He requested that readers respond to his thoughts about religion and literature with "seasoned reflections" (3). A review of the following issues of the *Newsletter* reveals that evidently no such responses were forthcoming. Perhaps the readers were too busy with their own teaching to write replies. It seems more likely, however, that Dunn's theoretical outline seemed less than relevant to their immediate concerns. Perhaps he was right when he asserted that the pervasive New Critical approaches had alienated even Adventist English teachers from feeling comfortable with trying to link religion to the reading of so-called secular literature. Regardless, Seventh-day Adventist literature teachers are still waiting for the publication of a comprehensive theoretical basis that takes into consideration contemporary literary theory and that can undergird their approach to the teaching of and writing about literature. What is important to understand, however, is that thoughtful critical contributions of the sort initiated by Dunn in the 1970s would not only help establish a Seventh-day Adventist literary theory but also would enlarge an overall Christian theory of literature.

CHAPTER SEVEN
CONCLUSION

In this book, I have attempted to bring together some of the central Christian and Seventh-day Adventist responses to the integration of faith and the teaching of literature, with particular emphasis on what has been accomplished thus far and what remains to be done. Christian literary critics and literature teachers have provided solid principles for understanding how the reading of imaginative writing can play a central and indispensable role in the Christian life. Similarly, Seventh-day Adventist thinkers and writers have done a reasonably effective job of clarifying what Ellen White and others of her generation may have intended in their comments about which literature should and should not be read. Also, the long-time emphasis among Christian and Seventh-day Adventist literature teachers on writing about and teaching the Bible as literature has been beneficial in that it has continued to underscore the artistry of the greatest of all texts and its influence on later writers.

Yet, much remains to be done in establishing a positive and meaningful basis for the teaching and reading of literature from Christian and Seventh-day Adventist perspectives. In recent years, Christian critics have attempted to come to grips with the challenges of contemporary literary theory. What they have yet to accomplish, however, is the construction of a positive and coherent literary theory or movement that can stand shoulder to shoulder with other competing theories. It is particularly important for Seventh-day Adventist teachers of literature to realize that some contemporary literary theories present real threats and challenges to basic Christian faith. It has been all too easy for literature teachers to ignore the basic premises of recent literary theory as a part of their general willingness to separate their religious faith from their professional lives. Part of this stems from what Clarence Walhout has called the tendency of "Christians as well as non-Christians" to "perceive Christianity as a matter of private religious belief that is distinct from public matters of learning and research within academic disciplines"

("Introduction" vii-viii). In reality, however, contemporary theory, even though at its extreme clearly alien to basic Christian premises, also does provide opportunities for Christians to establish their own theologically-based theories of reading. Postmodernism, after all, honors interpretive communities as the establishers of meaning in texts, and there is no reason why Christians cannot develop their own literary theory as an appropriate response of a long-established interpretive community.

It may well be that Seventh-day Adventist literature teachers can contribute to the establishment of such Christian literary theory as well as to their own more specific version of that theory. It is my belief that such contributions should center on the central pillars of historic Christianity as well as on the more specific emphases of the Seventh-day Adventist Church, what Guy summarizes as the "Sabbath," the "Advent hope, the continuing ministry of Christ, human wholeness, and truth" (237). Carrying an emphasis on Christian and Seventh-day Adventist theology over to form the basis for literary theory is a difficult challenge, one that calls for careful and imaginative thinking. Such thinking cannot occur within a vacuum, however, and must be linked to a thorough knowledge of the various historical and contemporary literary theories. Unfortunately, many Seventh-day Adventist teachers and literature students do not find the study of literary theory very exciting and useful. One immediate challenge, then, is for literature departments to equip themselves with teachers who can make literary theory understandable and relevant to the artistic and religious concerns of their students—teachers who can underscore the contributions as well as the weaknesses of the various competing approaches.

Perhaps even more important, however, is the need for Seventh-day Adventist literature teachers to realize how their faith and their disciplines are not artificially separated but are indeed linked together by more than the private faith of a teacher who also must earn a living in the public atmosphere of the classroom. This book has attempted to underscore some of the dimensions of that linkage by reminding readers of God's approval of the human imagination and creativity as evidenced in the content and the form of the Scriptures as well as in the writings of thoughtful Christians throughout the ages. In the end, the most lasting contribution the Seventh-day Adventist teacher of literature can make is to communicate to students how the reading of literature can enrich one's faith and one's relationship to God. It is that integration which should be our private and professional goal.

WORKS CITED

Ackerman, James S., and Thayer S. Warshaw, eds. *The Bible as/in Literature.* Glenview, IL: Scott, Foresman, 1976.

Alter, Robert. *The Art of Biblical Narrative.* New York: Basic Books, 1981.

___. *The Art of Biblical Poetry.* New York: Basic Books, 1985.

___. Frank Kermode, eds. *The Literary Guide to the Bible.* Cambridge, MA: Belknap Press of Harvard University Press, 1987.

The American Heritage Dictionary of the English Language. Boston: American Heritage and Houghton Mifflin, 1969.

Basaninyenzi, Gatsinzi. "Teaching an Anti-Christian Text from a Christian Perspective: The Case of S. Beckett's *Waiting for Godot.*" *Christ in the Classroom: Adventist Approaches to the Integration of Faith and Learning.* Compiled by Humberto Rasi. Vol. 10. Silver Spring, MD: Institute for Christian Teaching, 1996. 63-73.

Bate, Walter Jackson. *Criticism: The Major Texts.* New York: Harcourt Brace Jovanovich, 1952.

Battle Creek College Calendar 1896. Battle Creek, MI: Battle Creek College, 1896.

Baym, Nina, et al., eds. *The Norton Anthology of American Literature.* Shorter 5th ed. New York: Norton, 1999.

Bell, G. H. *Studies in English and American Literature.* Chicago: Ainsworth & Company, 1900.

Bloom, Allan. *The Closing of the American Mind.* New York: Simon and Schuster, 1987.

Bloom, Harold. *The Western Canon: The Books and the Schools of the Ages.* New York: Harcourt Brace, 1994.

Bracher, Peter, and David L. Barr. "The Bible Is Worthy of Secular Study: The Bible in Public Education Today." *The Bible in American Education: From Source Book to Textbook.* Eds. David L. Barr and Nicholas Piediscalzi. Philadelphia, PA and Chico, CA: Fortress Press and Scholars Press, 1982. 165-97.

Bradley, W. P. "Ellen G. White and Literature." *Seventh-day Adventists on*

Literature. Ed. Robert Dunn. Riverside, CA: Department of English, Loma Linda University, 1974. 63-89.

Bressler, Charles E. *Literary Criticism: An Introduction to Theory and Practice*. 2nd ed. Upper Saddle River, NJ: Prentice Hall, 1999.

Cobb, L. W. *Give Attendance to Reading*. Portland, OR: L. W. Cobb, 1966.

Cowan, Louise, and Os Guinness, eds. *Invitation to the Classics*. Grand Rapids, MI: Baker Books, 1998.

Cox, James D. "The New Historicism." *Contemporary Literary Theory: A Christian Appraisal*. Eds. Clarence Walhout and Leland Ryken. Grand Rapids, MI: William B. Eerdmans, 1991. 252-70.

Danziger, Marlies K., and W. Stacy Johnson. *An Introduction to Literary Criticism*. Boston: D. C. Heath, 1961.

Davis, Delmer. "Hotbed of Immorality: Seventh-day Adventists and the Battle Creek Theater in the 1880s." *Adventist Heritage* 7 (1982): 20-33.

Department of Education, General Conference of Seventh-day Adventists. "Guide to the Teaching of Literature." 1971. Rpt. in *Language Matters: Notes Toward an Adventist English Program*. General Ed. Verne Wehtje. Nashville: Southern Publishing Assoc., 1978. 138-144. (See Appendix A of this present volume for another reprinting.)

Dunn, Robert P. "A Biblical Basis for English Teaching–I." *Adventist English Newsletter* 5 (Fall 1972): 3-7.

___. "A Biblical Basis for English Teaching–II." *Adventist English Newsletter* 6, 7 (Winter-Spring 1973): 3-8.

___. "A Biblical Basis for English Teaching–III." *Adventist English Newsletter* 8 (Fall 1973): 3-6.

___. "The Image of Faith in Literature and Life." *Seventh-day Adventists on Literature*. Ed. Robert Dunn. Riverside, CA: Department of English, Loma Linda University, 1974. 175-93.

___. "Introduction." *Seventh-day Adventists on Literature*. Ed. Robert Dunn. Riverside, CA: Department of English, Loma Linda University, 1974. 5-9.

___. "Twin Tasks of the English Teacher." *Language Matters: Notes Toward an Adventist English Program*. General Ed. Verne Wehtje. Nashville: Southern Publishing Assoc., 1978. 87-109.

Eliot, T. S. "Religion and Literature." *Religion and Modern Literature: Essays in Theory and Criticism*. Eds. G. B. Tennyson and Edward E. Ericson, Jr. Grand Rapids, MI: William B. Eerdmans, 1975. 21-30.

Foerster, Norman, et al., eds. *American Prose and Poetry*. 4th ed. Boston: Houghton Mifflin, 1957.

Frye, Northrop. *Anatomy of Criticism: Four Essays*. Princeton: Princeton University Press, 1971.

____. *The Educated Imagination*. Bloomington: Indiana University Press, 1964.

____. *The Great Code: The Bible and Literature*. New York: Harcourt Brace Jovanovich, 1981.

Gibbs, Paul T. "Literature in Adventist Schools." *Seventh-day Adventists on Literature*. Ed. Robert Dunn. Riverside, CA: Department of English, Loma Linda University, 1974. 113-30.

____. "Recommended Imaginative Reading for Secondary Schools." Ts. Adventist Heritage Center, James White Library, Andrews University, Berrien Springs, MI.

Graff, Gerald. *Professing Literature: An Institutional History*. Chicago: University of Chicago Press, 1987.

Gros Louis, Kenneth R. R., with James S. Ackerman and Thayer S. Warshaw, eds. *Literary Interpretations of Biblical Narratives*. Nashville: Abingdon Press, 1974.

____, with James S. Ackerman, eds. *Literary Interpretations of Biblical Narratives*. Vol. II. Nashville: Abingdon Press, 1982.

Guerin, Wilfred L., et al. *A Handbook of Critical Approaches to Literature*. 4th ed. New York: Oxford University Press, 1999.

Guy, Fritz. *Thinking Theologically: Adventist Christianity and the Interpretation of Faith*. Berrien Springs, MI: Andrews University Press, 1999.

Haluska, Jan. "The Bible and Literature." *Christ in the Classroom: Adventist Approaches to the Integration of Faith and Learning*. Compiled by Humberto Rasi. Vol. 26B. Silver Spring, MD: Institute for Christian Teaching, 2000. 361-403.

Hamm, Minon. "Anatomy of the Center: An Application of Some Concepts of Northrop Frye." Diss. George Peabody College for Teachers, 1975.

Harper Study Bible. Grand Rapids, MI: Zondervan Bible Publishers, 1965.

Hart, James D. *The Popular Book: A History of America's Literary Taste*. New York: Oxford University Press, 1950.

Henry, Iris. "Teaching Shakespeare within the Context of Christian Faith: A Case Study of *Macbeth*." *Christ in the Classroom: Adventist Approaches to the Integration of Faith and Learning*. Compiled by Humberto Rasi. Vol. 17. Silver Spring, MD: Institute for Christian Teaching, 1996. 135-54.

Hirsch, Jr., E. D. *Cultural Literacy: What Every American Needs to Know*. Boston: Houghton Mifflin, 1987.

Holmes, Arthur F. *The Idea of a Christian College*. Rev. ed. Grand Rapids, MI: William B. Eerdmans, 1987.

Jacobs, Alan. "Deconstruction." *Contemporary Literary Theory: A Christian Appraisal*. Eds. Clarence Walhout and Leland Ryken. Grand Rapids, MI: William B. Eerdmans, 1991. 172-98.

___. "Psychological Criticism: From the Imagination to Freud and Beyond." *Contemporary Literary Theory: A Christian Appraisal*. Eds. Clarence Walhout and Leland Ryken. Grand Rapids, MI: William B. Eerdmans, 1991. 94-124.

Jeffrey, David Lyle. *People of the Book: Christian Identity and Literary Culture*. Grand Rapids, MI: William B. Eerdmans, 1996.

Jones, Douglas A. "Why Study Literature?" *Journal of Adventist Education* 51 (April-May 1989): 18-21+.

Juel, Donald, with James S. Ackerman and Thayer S. Warshaw, eds. *An Introduction to New Testament Literature*. Nashville: Abingdon Press, 1978.

Karolides, Nicholas J., ed. *Reader Response in Secondary and College Classrooms*. 2nd ed. Mahwah, NJ: Lawrence Erlbaum Associates, 2000.

Kirszner, Laurie G., and Stephen R. Mandell. *Literature: Reading, Reacting, Writing*. Compact 3rd ed. Fort Worth: Harcourt Brace, 1997.

Longman III, Tremper. *Literary Approaches to Biblical Interpretation*. Grand Rapids, MI: Zondervan, 1987.

McClarty, Wilma. "Why Teach the Bible as Literature?" *Journal of Adventist Education* 51 (April-May 1989): 23+.

McGarrell, Shirley. "Differential Perceptions of English Teachers of Literature in Seventh-day Adventist Secondary Schools in Selected Regions of the Carribean." Diss. Andrews University, 2000.

___. "Faith and Fiction: An Inspiring Dilemma for Seventh-day Adventists." *Christ in the Classroom: Adventist Approaches to the Integration of Faith and Learning*. Compiled by Humberto Rasi. Vol. 14. Silver Spring, MD: Institute for Christian Teaching, 1993. 289-307.

Marsden, George M. *The Soul of the American University: From Protestant Establishment to Established Nonbelief*. New York: Oxford University Press, 1994.

Maxwell, Mervin C. *Tell It to the World: The Story of Seventh-day Adventists*. Rev. ed. Mountain View, CA: Pacific Press, 1977.

Moncrieff, Scott E. "Adventists and fiction: Another look." *Dialogue* 8 (1996): 9-12.

Moulton, Richard Green. *The Literary Study of the Bible*. Boston: D.C. Heath, 1895.

___. *The Modern Reader's Bible*. New York: Macmillan, 1907.

Murfin, Ross, and Supryia M. Ray. *The Bedford Glossary of Critical and Literary Terms*. Boston: Bedford Books, 1997.

1910-1911 Emmanuel Missionary College Bulletin. Berrien Springs, MI: Emmanuel Missionary College, 1910.

1919-1920 Emmanuel Missionary College Bulletin. Berrien Springs, MI: Emmanuel Missionary College, 1919.

Norton, David. *A History of the English Bible as Literature*. Cambridge: Cambridge University Press, 2000.

Olsen, Mahlon Ellsworth. "The Evolution of Biblical Prose." Diss. University of Michigan, 1909.

___. *The Prose of Our King James Version*. Washington, DC: Review and Herald Publishing Assoc., 1947.

Oxford English Dictionary. The Compact Edition. Vol. 1. New York: Oxford University Press, 1971.

Pickering, James H., and Jeffrey D. Hoeper. *Concise Companion to Literature*. New York: McMillen, 1981.

Quinn, Arthur H. *A History of American Drama from the Beginning to the Civil War*. New York: Appleton-Century-Crofts, 1943.

Reynaud, Daniel. "Literary Theory and Biblical Interpretation." *Christ in the Classroom: Adventist Approaches to the Integration of Faith and Learning*. Compiled by Humberto Rasi. Vol. 21. Silver Spring, MD: Institute for Christian Teaching, 1998. 279-92.

___. "Secular Theory and Religious Faith: How to Think Christian in a Postmodern Society." *Spectrum* 28 (Winter 2000): 4-11.

Richter, David H, ed. *The Criticial Tradition: Classic Texts and Contemporary Trends*. 2nd ed. Boston: Bedford Books, 1998.

___. ed. *Falling into Theory: Conflicting Views on Reading Literature*. Boston: Bedford Books of St. Martin's Press, 1994.

Rine, George Washington. "Nathaniel Hawthorne." *The Youth's Instructor* 4 Aug. 1898: 601-03.

___. "Poetry: Its Nature and Mission." *The Youth's Instructor* 2 June 1898: 434-35.

___. "Washington Irving." *The Youth's Instructor* 26 May 1898: 401-03.

Roberts, Edgar, and Henry Jacobs. *Literature: An Introduction to Reading and Writing*. Compact Edition. Upper Saddle River, NJ: Prentice Hall, 1998.

Ryken, Leland. "Afterword." *Contemporary Literary Theory: A Christian Appraisal*. Eds. Clarence Walhout and Leland Ryken. Grand Rapids, MI: William B. Eerdmans, 1991. 292-302.

___. "Formalist and Archetypal Criticism." *Contemporary Literary Theory: A Christian Appraisal*. Eds. Clarence Walhout and Leland Ryken. Grand Rapids, MI: William B. Eerdmans, 1991. 1-23.

___. *The Liberated Imagination: Thinking Christianly about the Arts*. Wheaton: IL: Harold Shaw, 1989.

___. *The Literature of the Bible*. Grand Rapids, MI: Zondervan, 1974.

___. *Triumphs of the Imagination: Literature in Christian Perspective*. Downers Grove, IL: InterVarsity, 1979.

___. *Windows on the World: Literature in Christian Perspective*. 2nd ed. Dallas: Probe Books, 1990.

___. *Words of Delight: A Literary Introduction to the Bible*. Grand Rapids, MI: Baker Books, 1987.

___. *Words of Light: A Literary Introduction to the New Testament*. Grand Rapids, MI: Baker Books, 1987.

Sample, Carol. "The Salvation Theme in Flannery O'Connor." *Christ in the Classroom: Adventist Approaches to the Integration of Faith and Learning*. Compiled by Humberto Rasi. Vol. 3. Silver Spring, MD: Institute for Christian Teaching, 1991. 121-38.

Sayers, Dorothy. "The Image of God." *Christian Letters to a Post-Christian World: A Selection of Essays by Dorothy Sayers*. Selected and introduced by Roderick Jellema. Grand Rapids, MI: William B. Eerdmans, 1969. 100-06.

Searle, John. "The Storm over the University." *Falling into Theory: Conflicting Views on Reading Literature*. Ed. David H. Richter. Boston: Bedford Books of St. Martin's Press, 1994.

Sire, James W. *The Universe Next Door: A Basic Worldview Catalog*. 3rd ed. Downers Grove, IL: InterVarsity Press, 1997.

Stafford, Ottilie. "At the Center of Development." *Language Matters: Notes Toward an Adventist English Program*. General Ed. Verne Wehtje. Nashville: Southern Publishing Assoc., 1978. 9-19.

Taylor V, John Wesley. "Mahlon Ellsworth Olsen: Educational Ideas and Life Sketch." Ts. Adventist Heritage Center, James White Library, Andrews University, Berrien Springs, MI.

Tippett, H. M. "A Review of Some Principles in Dealing with Fiction and Imaginative Forms of Literature in Our Schools." *Seventh-day Adventists on Literature*. Ed. Robert Dunn. Riverside, CA: Dept. of English, Loma Linda University, 1974. 91-6.

Tyson, Lois. *Critical Theory Today: A User-Friendly Guide*. New York: Garland, 1999.

Vande Kopple, William J. "Toward a Christian View of Language." *Contemporary Literary Theory: A Christian Appraisal*. Eds. Clarence Walhout and Leland Ryken. Grand Rapids, MI: Wlliam B. Eerdmans, 1991. 199-230.

Vanden Bosch, James. "Moral Criticism: Promises and Prospects." *Contemporary Literary Theory: A Christian Appraisal*. Eds. Clarence Walhout and Leland Ryken. Grand Rapids, MI: William B. Eerdmans, 1991. 24-71.

Vander Weel, Michael. "Reader-Response Theories." *Contemporary Literary Theory: A Christian Appraisal*. Eds. Clarence Walhout and Leland Ryken. Grand Rapids, MI: William B. Eerdmans, 1991. 125-48.

Velez-Sepulveda, David. "Literature and Life: Teaching Fictional Literature in Adventist Higher Education." Compiled by Humberto Rasi. Vol. 10. Silver Spring, MD: Institute for Christian Teaching, 1993. 269-88.

Waller, John O. "A Contextual Study of Ellen G. White's Counsel Concerning Fiction." *Seventh-day Adventists on Literature*. Ed. Robert Dunn. Riverside, CA: Dept. of English, Loma Linda University, 1974. 47-62.

___. "Some Eclectically Garnered Reflections Concerning the Moral Criticism of Prose Fiction." Ts. Adventist Heritage Center, James White Library, Andrews University, Berrien Springs, MI.

___. "Some Roots." *Language Matters: Some Notes Toward an Adventist English Program*. General Ed. Verne Wehtje. Nashville: Southern Publishing Assoc., 1978. 123-136.

Wehtje, Verne. "Preface." *Language Matters: Notes Toward an Adventist English Program*. General Ed. Verne Wehtje. Nashville: Southern Publishing Assoc., 1978.

White, Ellen G. *Counsels to Parents, Teachers, and Students Regarding Christian Education*. Mountain View, CA: Pacific Press, 1943.

___. *Education*. Mountain View, CA: Pacific Press, 1952.

___, compiler. *Sabbath Readings for the Home Circle*. Nashville: M. A. Vroman, 1905.

___. *The Story of Patriarchs and Prophets*. Mountain View, CA: Pacific Press, 1958.

___. *Testimonies for the Church*. Vol. 4. Mountain View, CA: Pacific Press, 1948.

Wind, James P. *The Bible and the University: The Messianic Vision of William Rainey Harper*. Atlanta: Scholars Press, 1987.

RECOMMENDED READING

Resources for the Seventh-day Adventist Literature Teacher

The following list of works is not intended to be inclusive. Rather, I have chosen certain key works, many of them referred to rather continuously throughout the text of the present book, which have been particularly useful to me both in and out of the classroom over my years of teaching. As in the book itself, the list grows out of my own American educational and teaching career, but may prove useful to teachers of literature in other cultures and languages. Some of the books on the list are most readily available at university and research libraries, since they are no longer in print and available through their publishers.

General Works about Literature and Literary Theory/Criticism

Bressler, Charles E. *Literary Criticism: An Introduction to Theory and Practice.* 2nd ed. Upper Saddle River, NJ: Prentice Hall, 1999.

> This introductory work, intended as a college textbook, provides a good brief approach to the major literary theories, past to present.

Frye, Northrop. *The Educated Imagination.* Bloomington: Indiana University Press, 1964.

> In this short work intended for general audiences, Frye, one of the most distinguished twentieth-century literary critics, in clear and thought-provoking prose, makes the case for reading literature.

Graff, Gerald. *Professing Literature: An Institutional History.* Chicago: University of Chicago Press, 1987.

> Graff traces the development of and conflicts within English Departments and literature teaching in the United States with particular emphasis on how literary theory has helped to shape what literature teaching has become. He calls for an emphasis on teaching the conflicts so that students will be more aware of the theories that lurk behind classroom practices.

Guerrin, Wilfred L., et al. *A Handbook of Critical Approaches to Literature.* 4th ed. New York: Oxford University Press, 1999.

> A longtime and reliable introductory text for courses in critical theory and literary analysis, this book, besides providing good introductions to various literary approaches, includes sample essays on a few major works from a variety of theories.

Harmon, William, and C. Hugh Holman. *A Handbook to Literature*. 7th ed. Upper Saddle River, NJ: Prentice Hall, 1996.

Although there are a number of good literary dictionaries or handbooks, this one still provides the most solid and clear information about literary terms, genres, and other essential aspects of literature and literary study.

Richter, David H., ed. *The Critical Tradition: Classic Texts and Contemporary Trends*. 2nd ed. Boston: Bedford Books, 1998.

This text contains primary works of theory from ancient sources up to the present. Richter provides excellent introductions to the movements, trends, and featured writers included.

Richter, David H. *Falling into Theory: Conflicting Views on Reading Literature*. Boston: Bedford Books of St. Martin's Press, 1994.

One of the best works for involving students in the controversies among literary theorists, this book offers well-reasoned introductions by Richter along with selected essays by some of the most important contemporary writers about literature. Richter organizes the book around the following: "Why We Read"; "What We Read"; and "How We Read."

Tyson, Lois. *Critical Theory Today: A User-Friendly Guide*. New York: Garland, 1999.

An introductory text on recent critical theory, Tyson's book covers the competing theories in easy-to-follow prose and applies each theory to one work, F. Scott Fitzgerald's *The Great Gatsby*.

Christianity and Literature

Christianity and Literature. Conference on Christianity and Literature, published at the State University of West Georgia, Carrollton, GA, 30118.

Issued quarterly, this journal is "devoted to a scholarly exploration of how literature engages Christian thought, experience and practice." Without question, this publication offers Christian literature teachers their most important continuing resource.

Cowan, Louise, and Os Guinness, eds. *Invitation to the Classics*. Grand Rapids, MI: Baker Books, 1998.

This book provides "Christian" introductions to carefully chosen Western authors and works from Homer to such contemporary writers as Salman Rushdie.

Jeffrey, David Lyle. *People of the Book: Christian Identity and Literary Culture*. Grand Rapids, MI: William B. Eerdmans, 1996.

This ambitious book successfully engages contemporary theory from a Christian perspective, emphasizes that historical Christianity has generally not regarded biblical language and the biblical text in the way that some modern theorists have indicated, and underscores how a more balanced view of how Christianity has related to the Bible as text and language provides for a fuller understanding of how Christianity has enriched literary contributions throughout the centuries.

Religion and Literature. Department of English, University of Notre Dame, Notre Dame, IN 46556.

This scholarly journal casts a wider net than *Christianity and Literature* and includes research articles and book reviews related to how religion in its broadest sense and its many varieties intersects with literature.

Ryken, Leland. *Triumphs of the Imagination: Literature in Christian Perspective*. Downers Grove, IL: InterVarsity, 1979.

Although Ryken has authored a number of works centering on the arts and Christian faith, this work on literature remains the most useful for literature teachers because of its thorough development of ideas and its meaningful examples.

Ryken, Leland. *Windows on the World: Literature in Christian Perspective*. 2nd ed. Dallas: Probe Books, 1990.

Ryken treads much of the same ground in this work which he explores more thoroughly in *Triumphs of the Imagination*, but in this case he does so with less development and fewer specifics. The book is an excellent introduction for the general reader but less useful for the teacher.

Sayers, Dorothy. *Christian Letters to a Post-Christian World: A Selection of Essays by Dorothy Sayers*. Selected and introduced by Roderick Jellema. Grand Rapids, MI: William B. Eerdmans, 1969.

This book brings together the thoughtful responses of one of the twentieth-century's most thoughtful Christian writers on the relationship of religion to culture. Of particular importance, the work includes selections from Sayers's *The Mind of the Maker*, centering on how God's creative aspect is mirrored in humanity's creativity.

Tennyson, G. B., and Edward E. Ericson, Jr., eds. *Religion and Modern Literature: Essays in Theory and Criticism*. Grand Rapids, MI: William B. Eerdmans, 1975.

This anthology includes primary works by important writers about faith and literature, with particular emphasis on modern literature. Writers represented include T. S. Eliot, C. S. Lewis, and Flannery O'Connor.

Walhout, Clarence, and Leland Ryken, eds. *Contemporary Literary Theory: A Christian Appraisal*. Grand Rapids, MI: William B. Eerdmans, 1991.

Without question the most complete and thoughtful response by Christian literary critics to the issues raised by contemporary theory, this collection of essays is invaluable for anyone wishing to begin to understand how recent thinking about literature presents challenges as well as opportunities for Christian teachers of literature.

Seventh-day Adventists and Literature

The Adventist English Newsletter. A Publication of the Adventist English Teachers Association, presently edited by Dr. Bruce Closser, Andrews University, Berrien Springs, MI, 49104.

Although not published regularly during recent years, this periodical contains a variety of essays and short notes by Adventist English teachers, some of which relate specifically to the teaching of literature. There is no cumulative index to the contents, however, so articles of interest must be searched out by examining each number separately.

Dunn, Robert P., ed. *Seventh-day Adventists on Literature.* Riverside, CA: Department of English, Loma Linda University, 1974.

This work provides an excellent resource for teachers since it brings together primary materials by a variety of Seventh-day Adventist writers on faith and literature, including selections by L. W. Cobb, Harry M. Tippett, Paul Gibbs, and John Waller. Unfortunately, the book was issued in limited numbers and is not readily available except in library collections.

Rasi, Humberto, M., compiler. *Christ in the Classroom: Adventist Approaches to the Integration of Faith and Learning,* 26 vols. Silver Spring, MD: Institute for Christian Teaching, 1991– .

The results of regular seminars on the integration of faith and literature, the volumes in this series contain a number of essays written by Adventist literature teachers on a variety of literary topics. Recent volumes contain a cumulative index of all contributions, organized by general subject-matter headings.

Wehtje, Verne, general ed. *Language Matters: Notes Toward an Adventist English Program.* Nashville: Southern Publishing Assoc., 1978.

This book represents the most concerted effort to date among Seventh-day Adventist English teachers to present a meaningful explanation of their discipline purposes and content from a faith perspective. The chapters cover all areas of English teaching including composition and language study, but the writers place enough focus on literature (one complete chapter) to be a very helpful resource.

The Bible as Literature

Alter, Robert. *The Art of Biblical Narrative.* New York: Basic Books, 1981.

Alter, well-versed in Hebrew traditions and scholarship, presents insightful ideas about how Bible writers shaped their narratives.

Alter, Robert. *The Art of Biblical Poetry.* New York: Basic Books, 1985.

Alter's analysis of Hebrew poetry in the Bible is clear and persuasive.

Alter, Robert, and Frank Kermode, eds. *The Literary Guide to the Bible.* Cambridge, MA: Belknap Press of Harvard University Press, 1987.

Perhaps the best reference book for teachers of the Bible as literature, this work gathers essays on all aspects of the Bible and contains essential information for a literary understanding of the Scriptures.

Frye, Northrop. *The Great Code: The Bible and Literature.* New York: Harcourt Brace Jovanovich, 1981.

This is a demanding work which challenges the reader to see the essential unity of the Scriptures on several levels.

Gros Louis, Kenneth R. R., with James S. Ackerman and Thayer S. Warshaw, eds. *Literary Interpretations of Biblical Narratives*. Nashville: Abingdon Press, 1974.

This anthology grew out of the summer institutes on teaching the Bible as literature at Indiana University. The book includes insightful literary interpretations of several Old Testament stories.

Gros Louis, Kenneth R. R., with James S. Ackerman, eds. *Literary Interpretations of Biblical Narratives*. Vol. II. Nashville: Abingdon Press, 1982.

A continuation of the publications issued as a result of the summer institutes at Indiana University, this book also includes effective literary analyses of Old Testament stories.

Juel, Donald, with James S. Ackerman and Thayer S. Warshaw, eds. *An Introduction to New Testament Literature*. Nashville: Abingdon Press, 1978.

Another of the publications from the Indiana University summer institutes, this work concentrates on New Testament literature.

Longman III, Tremper. *Literary Approaches to Biblical Interpretation*. Grand Rapids, MI: Zondervan, 1987.

This short work provides an excellent introduction to how the Bible might be approached through reliance on contemporary literary theories.

Norton, David. *A History of the English Bible as Literature*. Cambridge: Cambridge University Press, 2000.

This book traces how the English Bible, particularly the King James (or Authorized Version), became so central in its influence on writers and readers as the repository of the best and most revered English style and language use.

Ryken, Leland. *Words of Delight: A Literary Introduction to the Bible*. Grand Rapids, MI: Baker Books, 1987.

Ryken's introduction to the literary aspects of the Old Testament is unsurpassed in its clarity and accessability for students. His analyses combine elements of formalism and archetypal criticism along with a relatively traditional Christian perspective.

Ryken, Leland. *Words of Light: A Literary Introduction to the New Testament*. Grand Rapids, MI: Baker Books, 1987.

As with his *Words of Delight*, this brief exploration of New Testament works provides effective literary analyses with Ryken's usual insightful Christian understandings. Ryken's handling of the Gospels and the Book of Revelation is particularly helpful for students in introductory courses.

GUIDE TO THE TEACHING OF LITERATURE IN SEVENTH-DAY ADVENTIST SCHOOLS[49]

(prepared by the Department of Education, General Conference of Seventh-day Adventists, 1971)

Introduction

The question of literature and its use in the Seventh-day Adventist classroom is perennially discussed at teachers' conventions and especially among those in whose classes it is presented. In an attempt to further clarify the church's position, a committee representative of the various segments of Adventist education spent a full week in study of the topic.

The statement prepared by this committee was recommended to the General Conference Department of Education and to the Autumn Council, where after some minor changes, it was accepted and referred back to the Department of Education for implementation.

The contents of these "Guidelines" are based on the accepted statement, and are intended to give direction to the teaching of literature in our schools.

"The great aim of the teacher should be the perfecting of Christian character in himself and in his students. Teachers, let your lamps be trimmed and burning, and they will not only be lights to your students, but will send out clear and distinct rays to the homes and neighborhoods where your students live, and far beyond into the moral darkness of the world."
–*Counsels to Parents and Teachers*, page 68.

Charles B. Hirsch, *Secretary*
Department of Education

---

[49]The "Guide," published in 1971, in its use of non-inclusive language ("he," "his," "him," and "man" to refer generically to members of both genders), mirrors typical editorial policies of the times. In 1971, even the National Council of Teachers of English had not yet adopted its non-sexist language guidelines for publishers in North America.

I. Philosophy

Literature in general sets forth man's impressions of his world, as well as his aspirations, deeds, thoughts, and accomplishments, whether good or bad. Literature selected, in particular for Seventh-day Adventist schools, should lead to the development of the whole man. It may be expressed through poetry or prose; it may be factual or non-factual; it may be drawn from secular or religious sources. It will give a comprehensive view of the universe, help solve fundamental problems, and answer questions on the origin, nature, and destiny of man while emphasizing the true, the honest, and the beautiful.

The study of literature should support the fundamental premise that God is the Creator and Sustainer of the earth and the entire universe and is the Source of all knowledge and wisdom. The presentation of literature should confirm the truth that God created man in His image and help restore that image by developing faith in Christ. It should nurture an intelligent dedication to the work of God and develop a desire to serve mankind.

Seventh-day Adventist educational philosophy holds that acquaintance with God can best be obtained through divine revelations of His nature and purposes. The objectives of the teaching of literature in Seventh-day Adventist schools will therefore be in harmony with those revelations, particularly as vouchsafed in Holy Scripture and emphasized in the writings of Ellen G. White.

The teaching of literature in Seventh-day Adventist schools should give primary emphasis to character-building. It should transmit to the students the spiritual ideals, beliefs, attitudes, and values of the church, and furthermore should encourage them to be thoughtful, law-abiding citizens as well as loyal, conscientious Christians.

Careful study of Ellen G. White's counsels and her total relationship to reading principles indicates that guided study of secular literature, both the fact-based and some true-to-principle non-fact based, is legitimate for Seventh-day Adventist schools. It should be studied with a sober regard to the positive principles set forth in Mrs. White's writings.

Acceptable literature, whatever its form, is serious art and should be taught in such a manner that students will become vividly aware of its aesthetic qualities—its beauty of word and structure, of rhythm and rhyme, of light and shade. The teacher should share with his students an innate and cultivated love of the best in literature that they might learn to appreciate the highest and to employ its principles in their own literary endeavors.

II. Selection of Literature for Seventh-day Adventist Schools

A. *Function*

The function of literature selected for study in Seventh-day Adventist schools is to acquaint the student with the artistic wealth available in all forms of the written word. Literature is designed to provide significant, artistic, lasting insights into essential human experience. It develops an appreciation and emulation of the beauty of language and the art of literary structure. The study of literature confronts the student with reality, explores significant questions, and introduces ideas in their historical context. It provides a basis for developing discriminatory powers and encourages the students to emulate the skills demonstrated by selections studied. It should tend to draw the reader to Christ, build up and strengthen understanding and faith, and help him to become a whole spiritual man.

B. *Criteria*

1. General

Literature assigned in Seventh-day Adventist schools should:

    a. Be serious art. It will lead to significant insight into the nature of man in society and will be compatible with Seventh-day Adventist values.

    b. Avoid sensationalism (the exploitation of sex or violence) and maudlin sentimentality (the exploitation of softer feelings to the detriment of a sane and level view of life).

    c. Not be characterized by profanity or other crude and offensive language.

    d. Avoid elements that give the appearance of making evil desirable or goodness appear trivial.

    e. Avoid simplified, excitingly suspenseful, or plot-dominated stories that encourage hasty and superficial reading.

    f. Be adapted to the maturity level of the group or individual.

2. Fiction

Webster's New International Dictionary of the English Language, Second Edition, Unabridged, defines *fiction* broadly as: "That which is feigned, invented or imagined; esp., a feigned or invented story, whether uttered or written with intent to deceive or not; –opposed to fact or reality. Fictitious literature; all works of imagination in narrative or dramatic form; specif., novels & romances...." In the minds of many the term *fiction* denotes less broadly the perverted, harmful form of imaginative writings often designed to exalt sin and sordidness. In most literary circles the term *fiction* has been understood merely to mean the categories of the novel and the short story.

From an intensive examination of her references to fiction, it appears that Ellen G. White used the term *fiction* to apply to works with the following characteristics: (1) It is addictive. (2) It may be sentimental, or sensational, erotic, profane, or trashy. (3) It is escapist, causing the reader to revert to a dream world and to be less able to cope with the problems of everyday life. (4) It unfits the mind for serious study, and devotional life. (5) It is time consuming and valueless.

Ellen G. White, while characterizing objectionable literature, recognized a proper limited use of certain non-factual materials by her endorsement of *Pilgrim's Progress* and by including in her compilation of *Sabbath Readings* (1877-1878) such materials in the form of simple stories teaching "moral and religious" lessons "that defend a sound morality and breathe a spirit of devotion, tenderness and true piety," at the same time specifying their value in contrast with "religious fiction" which had proved to be a curse.

In the selection of literary material the counsel of Ellen White should be followed in avoiding materials marked by the characteristics she attributed to fiction. Within these limitations some non-factual works, catalogued commonly as fiction, might be appropriately taught.

3. Biographies

Biographies may include the lives of persons whose religious views or personal lives are unworthy of emulation, as well as much novel or imaginative presentation.

All biographical selections are to be chosen with caution, and the same guidelines as recommended for other reading material be followed.

4. Glorification of Authors

The inspired word of the Spirit of Prophecy has given counsel to refrain from glorifying the authors of literary works (see *Counsels to Writers and Editors*, pp. 173, 174). It is recognized that certain undevout and ungodly authors have sometimes embodied in their writings some things which express cultural, moral, and aesthetic values, and, "We can trace the line of the world's teachers as far back as human records extend; but the Light was before them. As the moon and the stars of our solar system shine by the reflected light of the sun, so, as far as their teaching is true, do the world's great thinkers reflect the rays of the Sun of Righteousness. Every gleam of thought, every flash of the intellect, is from the Light of the world." *–Education*, pp. 13, 14.

Since the admonition has been given to teach students how to choose the good, and refuse the evil, in the teaching of literature primary emphasis should be placed upon the values, insights, and understanding to be found in the literature itself, avoiding the glorification of authors in any way.

5. Relevance

Present-day students are particularly concerned that their studies should be relevant to their experience and interests. Recognizing that, besides its traditionally appreciated values, literary study can promote understanding that may be useful for problem solving and for coping with personal and cultural change. The following criteria should be considered:

a. Teachers of literature in Adventist schools should build on the premise that both selection of materials and methods of teaching be governed by relevance to the development of students into mature Adventist Christians, committed to the search for wisdom and truth and concerned with the physical and spiritual well-being of their fellow men.

b. Teachers of literature should assist students to discover the relevance of the literature of the Bible and the writings of Ellen G. White to present-day concerns.

c. Adventist schools (particularly on the higher level), recognizing students' interest in currently pressing human problems, may include in their literature program such materials as encourage sharpened perceptions and fresh insights and challenge values that students have accepted or held without critical examination. The teacher's judicious attitude toward such material and candid explanation should reveal to students its usefulness for such higher values as perception and insight despite certain drawbacks. The teachers should inform administrators about the purposes and approaches involved in the use of such material. Appropriateness of topics and materials to the age of the student and harmony with the philosophy expressed in this document must always be important considerations.

6. Individual Student Conviction

In view of the fact that some students come to SDA classrooms with deep conscientious convictions about the kinds of assignments they may or may not accept, every effort should be made by all teachers of literature to provide optional acceptable reading on related topics for those students so that no one be embarrassed because of his individual interpretation of Spirit of Prophecy quotations.

C. Role of the Teacher

The teacher of literature in a Seventh-day Adventist school will be thoroughly dedicated to the beliefs and ideals of the church and will exemplify these in his personal and professional life. He will be concerned with the salvation of his students and the glorification of God. The teacher will use materials and methods to assist students in attaining the highest goals God has designed for man. He will be selective in his choice of assignments, and his methods of teaching will instill in each student those principles set forth in the Bible and the writings of Ellen G. White. He will remember that truth is best communicated in a setting of love, compassion, beauty, and simplicity. He will take into consideration the Adventist constituency in which he teaches, the homes from which the students come, most importantly the students themselves, adapting to their needs.

In attempting to solve his professional problems, the teacher should counsel with his colleagues, and in case of doubt on certain reading material to be presented to or read by the students, he should seek further counsel from the school administration.

III. Literature Representative of Multi-ethnic Groups

In the use of literature produced by such writers:

1. The teacher should become aware of the cultural characteristics of the students and should know his own reactions as a teacher by probing his own feelings and prejudices.
2. The teacher should strive for realistic communication through discussions of real life situations rather than placing undue emphasis upon the importance of grammar, pronunciation and other language mechanics.
3. There should be an awareness of the aptitudes and interests of students from multi-ethnic groups that enable the teacher to lift the aspirations of the student and lead him to achieve his highest potential.

4. The student shall be encouraged to feel that his heritage is an important contribution to society; therefore, he should not be embarrassed if he wishes to retain the distinguishing features of his own cultural background.

5. The teacher should himself communicate with the students on a one-to-one basis, stimulate free exchange of ideas, and help each class member to become a self-realizing productive member of society.

6. The scope and sequence of the curriculum materials in literature should reflect the pluralistic character of our society in such a way as to be multi-ethnically inclusive.

"Teacher, weed from your talks all that is not of the highest and best quality. Keep before the students those sentiments only that are essential."
–*Counsels to Parents and Teachers*, page 403.

THE INSTITUTE FOR CHRISTIAN TEACHING

The Institute for Christian Teaching (ICT) was established in 1987, through the generous donation of a committed Christian businessman, to promote excellence in Adventist education. Under the supervision of the Education Department of the General Conference of Seventh-day Adventists, the Institute offers seminars and develops resources to foster the integration of faith and learning in Christian schools, colleges, and universities.

Since 1988 and with additional funding from the General Conference of Seventh-day Adventists and other donors, the Institute has sponsored international faith and learning seminars for educators in the United States as well as in Argentina, Australia, Austria, Bolivia, Brazil, Colombia, Cote d'Ivoire, England, France, India, Jamaica, Kenya, Korea, Nigeria, Peru, Philippines, Singapore, South Africa, and Thailand.

The Institute for Christian Teaching pursues the following objectives:

1. To promote excellence—professional and spiritual—in Seventh-day Adventist teaching at the secondary and post-secondary levels.
2. To foster the integration of faith and learning throughout the curriculum on the basis of a biblical-Christian worldview.
3. To focus on the uniqueness, values, and implications of Seventh-day Adventist educational philosophy.
4. To stimulate research and publication in the area of Christ-centered, Bible-based, and service-oriented education.

At present, the Institute has available curricular guides for 16 secondary-school subjects in English, French, and Spanish. It also has published 500 essays on secondary, college/university, and professional topics developed by participants in the faith-and-learning seminars. These can be obtained individually or in bound volumes in the Christ in the Classroom series. Several of these essays are also available at www.aiias.edu/ict and at online.aiias.edu/ict

For a free catalogue of the materials available and information on upcoming seminars, contact:

The Institute for Christian Teaching
Department of Education
General Conference of Seventh-day Adventists
12501 Old Columbia Pike
Silver Spring, MD 20904-6600, U.S.A.
Telephone: (301) 680-5060
Fax: (301) 622-9627
E-mail: rodrigueze@gc.adventist.org

Appendix C

THE CENTER FOR COLLEGE FAITH

The Center for College Faith is an initiative of Andrews University which seeks to help faculty better understand and foster the faith development of college undergraduates. Membership in the Center is open to all Andrews University faculty and is voluntary. The Center was formally organized in 1998, but its origin lies in a faculty convocation in 1996 which recognized a need to more effectively highlight faith development as central to the entire undergraduate experience.

The stated mission of the Center is twofold. First, we seek to acquire and disseminate knowledge about how college students develop in their Christian beliefs, values, and lifelong commitment to God, especially in relation to direct academic experiences. Second, we endeavor to promote on the Andrews University campus the growth of a distinctly Christian undergraduate "culture of learning" informed by careful scholarship.

Funded by generous donors, the Center has co-sponsored (with the Institute for Christian Teaching) the Faith and Learning Conference at Andrews University in 1999 and the publication of the present volume. Ongoing plans include an active research initiative focused on the college impact on spiritual formation of undergraduates; a development program for Center faculty which supports professional growth, scholarship, and curricular revision pertinent to the Center's mission; a faculty seminar series to promote dialog on issues of faith development; and the support for publishing scholarship at the interface of Christian faith and the Academy.

For further information, please contact one of the co-directors of the Center:

Mickey D. Kutzner
Physics Department
Andrews University
Berrien Springs, MI 49104
(269) 471-6291
kutzner@andrews.edu

Randall J. Siebold
Department of Teaching and Learning
Andrews University
Berrien Springs, MI 49104
(269) 471-6235
randy@andrews.edu

INDEX